# 50 Mexican Premium Food Recipes for Home

By: Kelly Johnson

# Table of Contents

- Mole Poblano
- Chiles en Nogada
- Tacos al Pastor
- Carnitas
- Barbacoa
- Ceviche de Camarón
- Pozole Rojo
- Cochinita Pibil
- Enchiladas Suizas
- Tamales de Rajas con Queso
- Mole Verde
- Tinga de Pollo
- Sopes de Carne Asada
- Pescado a la Veracruzana
- Chilaquiles Rojos
- Arroz con Pollo
- Flautas de Pollo
- Huachinango a la Veracruza
- Gorditas de Chicharrón Prensado
- Tostadas de Atún
- Camarones al Ajillo
- Cactus Salad (Nopales)
- Chiles Rellenos de Queso
- Caldo de Res
- Pambazos
- Huaraches de Carne Asada
- Enchiladas de Mole
- Salsa Verde Cruda
- Tacos de Pescado
- Pibil Tacos
- Mexican Street Corn (Elote)
- Tamale Pie

- Mexican Beef Stew
- Churros con Chocolate
- Tres Leches Cake
- Coconut Flan
- Mexican Hot Chocolate
- Chicken Pozole
- Queso Fundido con Chorizo
- Mexican Rice
- Refried Beans
- Salsa Roja
- Pico de Gallo
- Albondigas (Mexican Meatballs)
- Chimichangas
- Mexican Cornbread
- Enchilada Sauce
- Mexican Stuffed Peppers
- Baked Mexican Chicken
- Mexican Shrimp Cocktail

**Mole Poblano**

**Ingredients:**

**For the Mole Sauce:**

- 4 dried mulato chiles
- 4 dried pasilla chiles
- 2 dried ancho chiles
- 1 tablespoon sesame seeds
- 1/4 cup almonds (or peanuts)
- 1/4 cup raisins
- 1/4 cup pumpkin seeds (pepitas)
- 1/4 cup corn tortillas, torn into pieces
- 1 medium onion, chopped
- 3 cloves garlic, minced
- 2 tablespoons vegetable oil
- 2 cups chicken or vegetable broth
- 1 cup crushed tomatoes
- 2 tablespoons cocoa powder (unsweetened)
- 2 tablespoons chocolate (Mexican chocolate or semisweet)
- 1 tablespoon ground cumin
- 1 teaspoon ground cinnamon
- 1/2 teaspoon ground cloves
- 1/2 teaspoon dried oregano
- 2 tablespoons sugar (optional, adjust to taste)
- Salt, to taste
- 2 tablespoons all-purpose flour (optional, for thickening)

**For the Chicken:**

- 2 lbs (900g) bone-in, skinless chicken thighs or breasts
- Salt and pepper, to taste
- 1 tablespoon vegetable oil

**For Garnishing:**

- Sesame seeds, toasted
- Fresh cilantro, chopped

**Instructions:**

1. **Prepare the Chiles:**

- Remove the stems and seeds from the dried chiles. Toast the chiles in a dry skillet over medium heat until they become fragrant, about 1-2 minutes per side. Be careful not to burn them.
- Place the toasted chiles in a bowl and cover with hot water. Let them soak for about 20 minutes, or until softened. Drain and discard the soaking water.

2. **Prepare the Mole Ingredients:**
   - In the same skillet, toast the sesame seeds, almonds (or peanuts), and pumpkin seeds until lightly browned and fragrant. Set aside.
   - Tear the corn tortillas into pieces and toast them in the skillet until crispy. Set aside.
   - Heat 2 tablespoons of vegetable oil in a large pot over medium heat. Add the chopped onion and cook until softened and translucent, about 5 minutes. Add the minced garlic and cook for another minute.

3. **Blend the Mole Sauce:**
   - In a blender or food processor, combine the soaked chiles, toasted sesame seeds, almonds, raisins, pumpkin seeds, and crispy tortillas. Blend until smooth, adding a little chicken or vegetable broth if needed.
   - Add the crushed tomatoes, cocoa powder, chocolate, ground cumin, ground cinnamon, ground cloves, dried oregano, and sugar (if using) to the blender. Blend until well combined.

4. **Cook the Mole Sauce:**
   - In the same pot used for the onions and garlic, add a little more vegetable oil if needed and pour in the mole mixture. Cook over medium heat for about 10 minutes, stirring frequently to prevent sticking.
   - Gradually add the chicken or vegetable broth, stirring continuously to achieve a smooth consistency. Simmer the sauce for about 20-30 minutes, until it thickens and the flavors meld together. If the sauce is too thin, you can mix 2 tablespoons of flour with a little water to form a slurry and stir it into the sauce to thicken.

5. **Prepare the Chicken:**
   - Season the chicken pieces with salt and pepper. Heat 1 tablespoon of vegetable oil in a large skillet over medium-high heat.
   - Add the chicken and cook until browned on all sides and cooked through, about 5-7 minutes per side. Remove from heat and set aside.

6. **Combine and Serve:**
   - Slice the cooked chicken and place it in a serving dish. Pour the hot mole sauce over the chicken.
   - Garnish with toasted sesame seeds and chopped fresh cilantro.

**Tips:**

- **Adjusting Flavor:** Taste the mole sauce and adjust seasoning with more salt, sugar, or chocolate as desired.
- **Make-Ahead:** Mole Poblano can be made ahead and stored in the refrigerator for up to 5 days or frozen for up to 3 months. Reheat gently before serving.
- **Serving Suggestions:** Mole Poblano pairs well with rice, beans, and warm tortillas.

Enjoy the deep, complex flavors of this traditional Mexican Mole Poblano!

# Chiles en Nogada

## Ingredients:

### For the Chiles:

- 6 large poblano chiles
- 1 tablespoon vegetable oil

### For the Picadillo (Filling):

- 1 lb (450g) ground pork (or a mix of pork and beef)
- 1 tablespoon vegetable oil
- 1 medium onion, finely chopped
- 2 cloves garlic, minced
- 1 large tomato, finely chopped
- 1 cup diced apples (such as Granny Smith or Fuji)
- 1/2 cup diced peaches (fresh or canned)
- 1/4 cup diced plantain (optional)
- 1/4 cup almonds, chopped
- 1/4 cup raisins
- 1/4 cup chopped candied citron (optional)
- 1/4 cup chopped fresh parsley
- 1/2 teaspoon ground cinnamon
- 1/2 teaspoon ground cloves
- 1/2 teaspoon ground cumin
- 1/2 cup beef or chicken broth
- Salt and freshly ground black pepper, to taste

### For the Nogada (Walnut Sauce):

- 2 cups walnuts, soaked in milk for 2 hours and drained
- 1 cup whole milk
- 1/4 cup sugar (adjust to taste)
- 1/2 teaspoon ground cinnamon
- 1 tablespoon sherry or brandy (optional)
- Salt, to taste

### For Garnishing:

- 1/2 cup pomegranate seeds
- Fresh parsley or cilantro, chopped

## Instructions:

1. **Prepare the Poblano Chiles:**
    - Preheat your oven's broiler or prepare a grill.
    - Roast the poblanos under the broiler or on the grill, turning occasionally, until the skins are blackened and blistered, about 5-7 minutes per side.
    - Place the roasted chiles in a plastic bag or cover them with a kitchen towel and let them steam for about 10 minutes. This helps loosen the skins.
    - Peel the skins off the chiles, being careful not to tear them. Remove the stems and seeds, and set the chiles aside.
2. **Prepare the Picadillo:**
    - In a large skillet or saucepan, heat 1 tablespoon of vegetable oil over medium heat.
    - Add the ground pork and cook, breaking it up with a spoon, until browned and cooked through.
    - Add the chopped onion and cook until softened, about 5 minutes. Stir in the minced garlic and cook for another minute.
    - Add the chopped tomato and cook for about 5 minutes, until the tomato is softened and the mixture is thickened.
    - Stir in the diced apples, peaches, plantain (if using), chopped almonds, raisins, candied citron (if using), and fresh parsley.
    - Season with ground cinnamon, ground cloves, ground cumin, salt, and freshly ground black pepper.
    - Pour in the beef or chicken broth, and simmer the mixture for about 10-15 minutes, until the flavors are well combined and the mixture is slightly thickened. Remove from heat and let cool.
3. **Prepare the Nogada (Walnut Sauce):**
    - Place the soaked and drained walnuts in a blender or food processor.
    - Add the whole milk, sugar, ground cinnamon, and sherry or brandy (if using). Blend until smooth and creamy. Adjust the seasoning with salt and more sugar, if needed.
4. **Assemble the Chiles en Nogada:**
    - Carefully stuff each poblano chile with the picadillo mixture.
    - Place the stuffed chiles on a serving platter.
5. **Serve:**
    - Pour the nogada (walnut sauce) generously over the stuffed chiles.
    - Garnish with pomegranate seeds and a sprinkle of fresh parsley or cilantro.

**Tips:**

- **Walnut Sauce:** For a smoother nogada, strain the walnut sauce through a fine sieve.
- **Make-Ahead:** The picadillo and nogada can be prepared in advance and refrigerated. Reheat the picadillo before stuffing the chiles and serve the nogada chilled or at room temperature.
- **Adjusting Sweetness:** The sweetness of the nogada can be adjusted to taste by adding more or less sugar.

Enjoy your Chiles en Nogada, a delicious and festive Mexican dish full of rich flavors and beautiful presentation!

**Tacos al Pastor**

**Ingredients:**

**For the Marinade:**

- 2 tablespoons dried guajillo chiles
- 2 tablespoons dried pasilla chiles
- 1 tablespoon dried ancho chiles
- 1/4 cup apple cider vinegar
- 1/4 cup orange juice
- 3 cloves garlic, minced
- 1 tablespoon achiote paste
- 1 tablespoon ground cumin
- 1 teaspoon ground oregano
- 1 teaspoon smoked paprika
- 1/2 teaspoon ground cloves
- 1/2 teaspoon ground cinnamon
- 1/2 teaspoon black pepper
- 2 tablespoons sugar (optional)
- Salt to taste

**For the Pork:**

- 2 lbs (900g) pork shoulder or pork loin, thinly sliced
- 1/2 cup pineapple, finely chopped (fresh or canned, drained)

**For Serving:**

- Corn or flour tortillas
- 1/2 cup pineapple, sliced or chopped
- 1/2 small red onion, finely chopped
- 1 cup fresh cilantro, chopped
- Lime wedges
- Salsa (such as Salsa Verde or Salsa Roja)

**Instructions:**

1. **Prepare the Marinade:**
    - Remove the stems and seeds from the dried chiles. Toast them in a dry skillet over medium heat for about 1-2 minutes, until they become fragrant. Be careful not to burn them.
    - Place the toasted chiles in a bowl and cover with hot water. Let them soak for about 20 minutes, or until softened. Drain and discard the soaking water.

- In a blender or food processor, combine the soaked chiles, apple cider vinegar, orange juice, minced garlic, achiote paste, ground cumin, ground oregano, smoked paprika, ground cloves, ground cinnamon, black pepper, and sugar (if using). Blend until smooth.
- Season the marinade with salt to taste.

2. **Marinate the Pork:**
   - Place the thinly sliced pork in a large bowl or resealable plastic bag.
   - Pour the marinade over the pork and toss to coat evenly. Refrigerate for at least 2 hours, or overnight for the best flavor.

3. **Cook the Pork:**
   - Preheat a grill or a large skillet over medium-high heat. If using a grill, ensure it is well-oiled to prevent sticking.
   - If using a skillet, heat 1 tablespoon of vegetable oil over medium-high heat.
   - Cook the marinated pork slices for about 4-6 minutes per side, or until well-cooked and slightly charred. If using a grill, cook until the edges are crispy and caramelized.
   - Remove the pork from the heat and let it rest for a few minutes before slicing it into small pieces.

4. **Prepare the Tacos:**
   - Warm the tortillas on the grill or in a dry skillet until they are soft and pliable.
   - Fill each tortilla with a portion of the cooked pork.
   - Top with fresh pineapple, finely chopped red onion, and chopped cilantro.

5. **Serve:**
   - Serve the tacos with lime wedges and your choice of salsa.

**Tips:**

- **Achiote Paste:** If you can't find achiote paste, you can substitute with a combination of paprika and a bit of soy sauce, though the flavor will be slightly different.
- **Pineapple:** Adding pineapple to the marinade gives the pork a subtle sweetness and helps tenderize the meat. For extra pineapple flavor, you can also grill the pineapple slices alongside the pork.
- **Make-Ahead:** The marinated pork can be prepared a day in advance and kept in the refrigerator. Cook it just before serving.

Enjoy your homemade Tacos al Pastor with all the traditional fixings for an authentic Mexican street food experience!

**Carnitas**

**Ingredients:**

- 3-4 lbs (1.4-1.8 kg) pork shoulder or pork butt, cut into large chunks
- 1 tablespoon vegetable oil
- 1 large onion, coarsely chopped
- 4 cloves garlic, minced
- 2-3 bay leaves
- 1 tablespoon ground cumin
- 1 tablespoon dried oregano
- 1 teaspoon smoked paprika
- 1 teaspoon ground coriander
- 1/2 teaspoon ground cloves
- 1/2 teaspoon ground black pepper
- 1 teaspoon salt (or to taste)
- 1 cup chicken broth
- 1/2 cup fresh orange juice
- 1/4 cup lime juice (about 2 limes)
- 1 cup fresh orange juice
- 1-2 teaspoons sugar (optional, adjust to taste)
- 2-3 tablespoons lard (optional, for crisping)

**For Serving:**

- Warm tortillas
- Sliced radishes
- Chopped cilantro
- Lime wedges
- Salsa or hot sauce
- Pickled jalapeños (optional)

**Instructions:**

1. **Prepare the Pork:**
   - Cut the pork shoulder into large chunks, about 2-3 inches in size. This will help the meat cook evenly and become tender.
2. **Sear the Pork:**
   - Heat the vegetable oil in a large Dutch oven or heavy-bottomed pot over medium-high heat.
   - Add the pork chunks in batches, making sure not to overcrowd the pot. Sear each side until browned, about 4-5 minutes per side. Remove the pork and set aside.

3. **Prepare the Flavor Base:**
   - In the same pot, add the chopped onion and cook until softened and translucent, about 5 minutes.
   - Stir in the minced garlic and cook for another minute until fragrant.
   - Add the bay leaves, ground cumin, dried oregano, smoked paprika, ground coriander, ground cloves, black pepper, and salt. Stir well to combine.
4. **Cook the Pork:**
   - Return the seared pork chunks to the pot. Stir to coat the pork with the spices and onion mixture.
   - Pour in the chicken broth, orange juice, and lime juice. The liquid should come about halfway up the pork.
   - Bring the mixture to a boil, then reduce the heat to low and cover. Simmer gently for 2-3 hours, or until the pork is very tender and easily shreds with a fork. You may need to add more broth or water if the liquid level gets too low.
5. **Crisp the Pork:**
   - Once the pork is tender, remove it from the pot and shred it using two forks. Discard any large pieces of fat or bones.
   - Heat 2-3 tablespoons of lard (or additional vegetable oil) in a large skillet over medium-high heat.
   - Add the shredded pork to the skillet and cook, stirring occasionally, until the edges are crispy and caramelized, about 10-15 minutes. You can also do this step in the oven by spreading the shredded pork on a baking sheet and broiling until crispy.
6. **Serve:**
   - Serve the crispy carnitas with warm tortillas, and top with sliced radishes, chopped cilantro, lime wedges, salsa or hot sauce, and pickled jalapeños if desired.

**Tips:**

- **Lard for Crisping:** Lard adds authentic flavor and helps achieve a crispy texture, but you can use vegetable oil if you prefer.
- **Flavor Adjustments:** Adjust the seasoning to taste, especially with salt and sugar, which balances the flavors.
- **Make-Ahead:** Carnitas can be made ahead of time and stored in the refrigerator for up to 4 days or frozen for up to 3 months. Reheat in a skillet to crisp up before serving.

Enjoy your delicious and flavorful Carnitas!

**Barbacoa**

**Ingredients:**

**For the Barbacoa:**

- 3-4 lbs (1.4-1.8 kg) beef chuck roast or beef cheeks, trimmed of excess fat
- 2 tablespoons vegetable oil
- 1 large onion, coarsely chopped
- 4 cloves garlic, minced
- 2-3 dried guajillo chiles
- 2-3 dried ancho chiles
- 1 dried pasilla chile
- 1 tablespoon ground cumin
- 1 tablespoon dried oregano
- 1 teaspoon smoked paprika
- 1/2 teaspoon ground cloves
- 1/2 teaspoon ground cinnamon
- 1/2 teaspoon black pepper
- 1 teaspoon salt (or to taste)
- 1/2 cup apple cider vinegar
- 1/2 cup beef broth (or more as needed)
- 1 tablespoon tomato paste
- 1-2 bay leaves
- 1-2 tablespoons lime juice (about 1 lime)
- 1/4 cup fresh cilantro, chopped (optional, for garnish)

**For Serving:**

- Warm tortillas
- Sliced onions
- Chopped cilantro
- Lime wedges
- Salsa or hot sauce
- Pickled jalapeños (optional)

**Instructions:**

1. **Prepare the Chiles:**
    - Remove the stems and seeds from the dried chiles. Toast them in a dry skillet over medium heat for about 1-2 minutes until they become fragrant, being careful not to burn them.
    - Place the toasted chiles in a bowl and cover with hot water. Let them soak for about 20 minutes, or until softened. Drain and discard the soaking water.

2. **Blend the Sauce:**
   - In a blender or food processor, combine the soaked chiles, ground cumin, dried oregano, smoked paprika, ground cloves, ground cinnamon, black pepper, salt, apple cider vinegar, beef broth, and tomato paste. Blend until smooth.
3. **Sear the Meat:**
   - Heat the vegetable oil in a large Dutch oven or heavy-bottomed pot over medium-high heat.
   - Add the beef chunks and sear on all sides until browned, about 4-5 minutes per side. Remove the beef from the pot and set aside.
4. **Cook the Barbacoa:**
   - In the same pot, add the chopped onion and cook until softened and translucent, about 5 minutes. Stir in the minced garlic and cook for another minute.
   - Return the seared beef to the pot. Pour the blended chile sauce over the beef, making sure it is well-coated.
   - Add the bay leaves and enough beef broth to cover the meat halfway.
   - Bring the mixture to a boil, then reduce the heat to low, cover, and simmer for 3-4 hours, or until the meat is very tender and shreds easily with a fork. Alternatively, you can cook it in a slow cooker on low for 8 hours.
5. **Shred the Meat:**
   - Once the meat is tender, remove it from the pot and shred it using two forks. Discard any large pieces of fat or bones.
   - Return the shredded meat to the pot and stir to combine with the cooking liquid. Simmer uncovered for an additional 10-15 minutes, allowing the flavors to meld and the sauce to reduce slightly.
6. **Serve:**
   - Serve the Barbacoa with warm tortillas and garnish with sliced onions, chopped cilantro, lime wedges, and your choice of salsa or hot sauce.
   - For an authentic touch, you can also serve it with pickled jalapeños.

## Tips:

- **Meat Cuts:** Beef chuck roast is commonly used, but beef cheeks or brisket can also be excellent choices for this recipe.
- **Adjusting Spice Levels:** Adjust the number of chiles and spices according to your heat preference.
- **Make-Ahead:** Barbacoa can be made ahead of time and stored in the refrigerator for up to 4 days or frozen for up to 3 months. Reheat thoroughly before serving.

Enjoy the flavorful and tender Barbacoa with all your favorite toppings and sides!

## Ceviche de Camarón

### Ingredients:

- 1 lb (450g) raw shrimp, peeled and deveined
- 1 cup fresh lime juice (about 8-10 limes)
- 1/2 cup fresh lemon juice (about 2 lemons)
- 1/2 cup orange juice (optional, for a touch of sweetness)
- 1 medium red onion, finely diced
- 1 medium tomato, diced
- 1 cucumber, peeled, seeded, and diced
- 1 jalapeño or serrano pepper, seeded and finely chopped (adjust to taste)
- 1/4 cup fresh cilantro, chopped
- 2-3 tablespoons olive oil
- 1 teaspoon salt (or to taste)
- 1/2 teaspoon black pepper (or to taste)
- 1 avocado, diced (optional, for garnish)
- Tortilla chips or tostadas, for serving

### Instructions:

1. **Prepare the Shrimp:**
   - Cut the raw shrimp into small, bite-sized pieces. If the shrimp are large, you may need to chop them into smaller pieces for better texture.
2. **Marinate the Shrimp:**
   - Place the chopped shrimp in a large, non-reactive bowl (such as glass or plastic).
   - Pour the lime juice, lemon juice, and orange juice (if using) over the shrimp, making sure they are fully submerged. The acidity from the citrus juices will "cook" the shrimp.
   - Cover the bowl with plastic wrap and refrigerate for about 1-2 hours, or until the shrimp turn opaque and are fully "cooked" in the citrus juice. Stir occasionally to ensure even marination.
3. **Prepare the Vegetables:**
   - While the shrimp is marinating, dice the red onion, tomato, and cucumber. Seed and finely chop the jalapeño or serrano pepper.
4. **Combine Ingredients:**
   - After the shrimp has marinated and turned opaque, drain off some of the excess citrus juice if there is too much liquid.
   - Add the diced red onion, tomato, cucumber, and chopped jalapeño to the bowl with the shrimp.
   - Stir in the chopped cilantro and olive oil. Season with salt and black pepper to taste.
5. **Garnish and Serve:**

- If using avocado, gently fold the diced avocado into the ceviche just before serving.
- Serve the Ceviche de Camarón chilled with tortilla chips or tostadas on the side. You can also serve it with additional lime wedges for extra tanginess.

**Tips:**

- **Freshness:** Use the freshest shrimp possible for the best flavor and texture.
- **Acidity:** Adjust the amount of citrus juice based on your taste preference. Some people like more or less acidity.
- **Spice Level:** Adjust the amount of jalapeño or serrano pepper to your desired heat level. You can also omit it if you prefer a milder ceviche.
- **Make-Ahead:** Ceviche is best enjoyed fresh, but you can prepare it a few hours in advance. Just make sure to keep it refrigerated until serving.

Enjoy your Ceviche de Camarón, a delicious and refreshing dish perfect for warm weather or as a vibrant appetizer!

**Pozole Rojo**

**Ingredients:**

**For the Pozole:**

- 2 lbs (900g) pork shoulder or pork butt, cut into large chunks
- 1 lb (450g) pork ribs or pork neck bones (optional, for added flavor)
- 1 tablespoon vegetable oil
- 1 large onion, coarsely chopped
- 4 cloves garlic, minced
- 6 cups chicken or vegetable broth
- 1 can (15 oz/425g) hominy (or about 4 cups homemade hominy), drained and rinsed
- 2-3 bay leaves
- 1 teaspoon dried oregano
- 1 teaspoon ground cumin
- Salt and freshly ground black pepper, to taste

**For the Red Chili Sauce:**

- 4-6 dried guajillo chiles
- 2-3 dried ancho chiles
- 2-3 dried pasilla chiles
- 2 cloves garlic, minced
- 1/2 cup chicken broth (or water)
- 1 tablespoon vegetable oil

**For Garnishing:**

- 1 small head of cabbage, finely shredded
- 1-2 radishes, thinly sliced
- 1 small red onion, thinly sliced
- 1/2 cup fresh cilantro, chopped
- Lime wedges
- Sliced jalapeños (optional)
- Avocado, diced (optional)
- Crispy tortilla strips or tostadas

**Instructions:**

1. **Prepare the Red Chili Sauce:**
   - Remove the stems and seeds from the dried chiles. Toast them in a dry skillet over medium heat for about 1-2 minutes, until fragrant, but be careful not to burn them.

- Place the toasted chiles in a bowl and cover with hot water. Let them soak for about 20 minutes, or until softened. Drain and discard the soaking water.
- In a blender or food processor, combine the soaked chiles, minced garlic, and 1/2 cup chicken broth. Blend until smooth. If the sauce is too thick, add a little more chicken broth or water.

2. **Cook the Pork:**
    - In a large pot or Dutch oven, heat the vegetable oil over medium-high heat.
    - Add the pork shoulder, ribs, or neck bones in batches, searing until browned on all sides. Remove the meat and set aside.
    - In the same pot, add the chopped onion and cook until softened, about 5 minutes. Stir in the minced garlic and cook for another minute.

3. **Combine Ingredients:**
    - Return the seared pork to the pot with the onions and garlic. Pour in the red chili sauce and stir well to combine.
    - Add the chicken or vegetable broth, bay leaves, dried oregano, and ground cumin. Bring the mixture to a boil, then reduce the heat to low.
    - Simmer uncovered for about 1.5 to 2 hours, or until the pork is tender and can be easily shredded. Skim off any foam or fat that rises to the surface.

4. **Add the Hominy:**
    - Stir in the drained and rinsed hominy. Continue to simmer for an additional 30 minutes to allow the flavors to meld and the hominy to heat through.
    - Season with salt and freshly ground black pepper to taste.

5. **Serve:**
    - Ladle the pozole into bowls. Serve with shredded cabbage, sliced radishes, sliced red onion, chopped cilantro, lime wedges, sliced jalapeños, and diced avocado on the side.
    - Provide crispy tortilla strips or tostadas for added crunch.

## Tips:

- **Hominy:** If using dried hominy, soak it overnight and cook according to the package instructions before adding it to the pozole.
- **Adjusting Spice Levels:** Adjust the number of chiles to control the heat level of the pozole.
- **Make-Ahead:** Pozole can be made a day in advance and stored in the refrigerator. The flavors will develop further as it sits. Reheat thoroughly before serving.

Enjoy your Pozole Rojo, a comforting and flavorful dish perfect for gatherings or cozy meals!

# Cochinita Pibil

**Ingredients:**

**For the Marinade:**

- 1/2 cup achiote paste (available at Latin markets or online)
- 1/2 cup fresh orange juice (about 2 oranges)
- 1/4 cup fresh lime juice (about 2 limes)
- 4 cloves garlic, minced
- 1 tablespoon ground cumin
- 1 tablespoon dried oregano
- 1 teaspoon ground cloves
- 1 teaspoon ground black pepper
- 1 teaspoon salt (or to taste)
- 1 tablespoon vegetable oil

**For the Pork:**

- 3-4 lbs (1.4-1.8 kg) pork shoulder or pork butt, cut into large chunks
- 1 large onion, coarsely chopped
- 2-3 bay leaves
- 4-6 banana leaves (or aluminum foil if banana leaves are unavailable)

**For Serving:**

- Corn tortillas or soft flour tortillas
- Pickled red onions
- Sliced radishes
- Fresh cilantro
- Lime wedges
- Salsa or hot sauce (optional)

**Instructions:**

1. **Prepare the Marinade:**
    - In a medium bowl, combine the achiote paste, fresh orange juice, fresh lime juice, minced garlic, ground cumin, dried oregano, ground cloves, black pepper, salt, and vegetable oil. Mix well to form a smooth marinade.
2. **Marinate the Pork:**
    - Place the pork chunks in a large bowl or resealable plastic bag.
    - Pour the marinade over the pork, ensuring that all pieces are well-coated. Cover the bowl or seal the bag and refrigerate for at least 4 hours, preferably overnight, to allow the flavors to infuse.

3. **Prepare the Cooking Vessel:**
   - If using banana leaves, briefly heat them over an open flame or in a dry skillet to make them pliable. This will help them wrap around the pork more easily.
   - Line a large baking dish or Dutch oven with the banana leaves, leaving some overhanging the edges.
4. **Cook the Pork:**
   - Preheat your oven to 300°F (150°C).
   - Remove the marinated pork from the refrigerator and place it in the lined baking dish or Dutch oven.
   - Scatter the chopped onion over the pork and tuck the bay leaves among the pork pieces.
   - Fold the overhanging banana leaves over the pork, covering it completely. If using aluminum foil, wrap the pork tightly in foil instead.
   - Cover the dish with a lid or additional foil to ensure it is sealed well.
5. **Bake the Pork:**
   - Place the covered dish in the preheated oven and bake for 4 to 5 hours, or until the pork is very tender and can be easily shredded with a fork. The slow cooking process will make the meat succulent and infused with the marinade.
6. **Shred the Pork:**
   - Once the pork is cooked, remove it from the oven and let it rest for a few minutes.
   - Transfer the pork to a large bowl and shred it using two forks. If desired, you can also lightly toss it with some of the cooking juices to enhance the flavor and moisture.
7. **Serve:**
   - Serve the Cochinita Pibil with warm corn or flour tortillas. Top with pickled red onions, sliced radishes, fresh cilantro, and lime wedges.
   - Add salsa or hot sauce if desired.

**Tips:**

- **Banana Leaves:** If banana leaves are not available, aluminum foil works as a substitute, though it won't impart the same subtle flavor.
- **Achiote Paste:** This ingredient is crucial for the authentic flavor of Cochinita Pibil. You can find it at Latin markets or online.
- **Make-Ahead:** The pork can be cooked ahead of time and kept in the refrigerator for up to 4 days. Reheat gently before serving.

Enjoy your Cochinita Pibil, a dish that brings the vibrant flavors of Yucatán cuisine right to your table!

**Enchiladas Suizas**

**Ingredients:**

**For the Enchiladas:**

- 12-16 corn or flour tortillas
- 2 cups cooked, shredded chicken (rotisserie chicken works well)
- 1 cup grated Swiss cheese (or Monterey Jack cheese)
- 1 cup sour cream or Mexican crema
- 1 tablespoon vegetable oil (for frying tortillas)
- Fresh cilantro, chopped (for garnish)
- Lime wedges (for serving)

**For the Green Sauce:**

- 1 lb (450g) tomatillos, husked and rinsed
- 2-3 green chiles (such as serrano or jalapeño), stems removed
- 1 small onion, coarsely chopped
- 2 cloves garlic
- 1 cup chicken or vegetable broth
- 1/2 teaspoon ground cumin
- 1/2 teaspoon dried oregano
- Salt and freshly ground black pepper, to taste
- 1 tablespoon vegetable oil

**Instructions:**

1. **Prepare the Green Sauce:**
   - **Roast the Tomatillos and Chiles:** Preheat your broiler or grill. Place the tomatillos and green chiles on a baking sheet and roast under the broiler, turning occasionally, until they are charred and blackened on the outside, about 5-10 minutes. Alternatively, you can roast them on a grill.
   - **Blend the Sauce:** Transfer the roasted tomatillos and chiles to a blender or food processor. Add the coarsely chopped onion and garlic. Blend until smooth.
   - **Cook the Sauce:** Heat the vegetable oil in a saucepan over medium heat. Pour in the blended mixture and cook, stirring occasionally, for about 5 minutes. Add the chicken or vegetable broth, ground cumin, dried oregano, salt, and black pepper. Simmer for another 10 minutes, until the sauce thickens slightly. Adjust seasoning to taste. Remove from heat and set aside.
2. **Prepare the Tortillas:**
   - **Fry the Tortillas:** Heat the vegetable oil in a skillet over medium heat. Briefly fry each tortilla for about 15-20 seconds on each side, just until soft and pliable. Drain on paper towels. (Alternatively, you can warm the tortillas in the oven or on a dry skillet if you prefer a healthier option.)

3. **Assemble the Enchiladas:**
    - Preheat your oven to 375°F (190°C).
    - Spread a small amount of the green sauce on the bottom of a baking dish to prevent sticking.
    - Dip each tortilla into the green sauce, then fill with a portion of shredded chicken. Roll up the tortilla and place it seam-side down in the baking dish. Repeat with the remaining tortillas and filling.
    - Pour the remaining green sauce over the top of the rolled tortillas, covering them completely.
    - Sprinkle the grated Swiss cheese evenly over the top.
4. **Bake the Enchiladas:**
    - Cover the baking dish with aluminum foil and bake for 20 minutes. Remove the foil and bake for an additional 10-15 minutes, or until the cheese is melted and bubbly and the sauce is hot throughout.
5. **Serve:**
    - Garnish the Enchiladas Suizas with chopped fresh cilantro and serve with lime wedges on the side. You can also add a dollop of sour cream or Mexican crema on top if desired.

**Tips:**

- **Cheese Choices:** Swiss cheese is traditional, but you can use other cheeses like Monterey Jack or cheddar if preferred.
- **Make-Ahead:** You can assemble the enchiladas ahead of time and refrigerate them. Bake them just before serving.
- **Vegetarian Option:** For a vegetarian version, substitute the chicken with cooked black beans or sautéed vegetables.

Enjoy your flavorful and creamy Enchiladas Suizas, a comforting and satisfying dish perfect for any occasion!

**Tamales de Rajas con Queso**

**Ingredients:**

**For the Tamales:**

- 2 cups masa harina (corn flour for tamales)
- 1 cup vegetable or chicken broth (or more as needed)
- 1/2 cup lard or vegetable shortening
- 1 teaspoon baking powder
- 1/2 teaspoon salt

**For the Filling:**

- 4-5 fresh poblano peppers
- 1 cup queso fresco, crumbled (or Monterey Jack, cheddar, or a combination)
- 1 small onion, finely chopped
- 2 cloves garlic, minced
- 1 tablespoon vegetable oil
- 1/2 teaspoon dried oregano
- 1/4 teaspoon ground cumin
- Salt and freshly ground black pepper, to taste

**For Assembling:**

- 24-30 dried corn husks (soaked in warm water for 30 minutes)
- Additional vegetable or chicken broth, as needed

**Instructions:**

1. **Prepare the Corn Husks:**
    - Soak the dried corn husks in warm water for at least 30 minutes to soften. Drain and pat dry with a towel. Keep the husks covered with a damp cloth to prevent them from drying out while you work.
2. **Prepare the Filling:**
    - **Roast the Poblanos:** Place the poblano peppers on a baking sheet and roast under a broiler, turning occasionally, until the skins are charred and blistered, about 5-10 minutes. Alternatively, you can roast them over an open flame or on a grill.
    - **Peel and Slice:** Transfer the roasted peppers to a plastic bag and let them steam for about 10 minutes. Peel off the charred skin, remove the seeds, and slice the peppers into thin strips.
    - **Cook the Filling:** Heat the vegetable oil in a skillet over medium heat. Add the chopped onion and cook until softened, about 5 minutes. Stir in the minced garlic and cook for another minute. Add the sliced poblano peppers, dried oregano, ground cumin, salt, and black pepper. Cook for another 5 minutes, until the

peppers are tender and well combined with the onion and garlic. Remove from heat and let cool slightly.
    - **Add Cheese:** Gently fold the crumbled queso fresco into the pepper mixture.
3. **Prepare the Tamale Dough:**
    - In a large bowl, combine the masa harina, baking powder, and salt. Mix well.
    - Add the lard or vegetable shortening to the masa harina and mix using your hands or a mixer until the mixture resembles coarse crumbs.
    - Gradually add the vegetable or chicken broth, mixing until the dough is smooth and has a soft, spreadable consistency. The masa dough should spread easily but not be too runny.
4. **Assemble the Tamales:**
    - Take a soaked corn husk and spread a portion of the masa dough (about 2 tablespoons) in the center of the husk, leaving about 1 inch on each side.
    - Add a spoonful of the poblano and cheese filling on top of the masa.
    - Fold the sides of the husk over the masa and filling, then fold up the bottom of the husk to enclose the tamale. The tamale should be tightly wrapped but not overly packed.
    - Repeat with the remaining husks, masa, and filling.
5. **Steam the Tamales:**
    - Arrange the tamales upright in a large steamer or tamale pot. If needed, place a folded cloth or small rack at the bottom to keep the tamales from touching the direct heat.
    - Cover the tamales with a damp cloth or additional corn husks.
    - Steam over medium heat for 1.5 to 2 hours, or until the masa is fully cooked and separates easily from the husks. Check the water level in the steamer periodically, adding more water as needed to keep the steam going.
6. **Serve:**
    - Let the tamales rest for about 10 minutes before serving. This helps the masa firm up and makes them easier to unwrap.
    - Serve with your favorite salsas, Mexican crema, or simply enjoy them on their own.

## Tips:

- **Masa Consistency:** The masa should be smooth and spreadable. If it feels dry, add more broth a little at a time. If it's too runny, add a bit more masa harina.
- **Flavor Variations:** You can add other ingredients to the filling, such as sautéed mushrooms, corn, or even cooked chicharrón prensado (pressed pork cracklings).
- **Freezing:** Tamales can be frozen after cooking. Cool them completely, then wrap tightly in plastic wrap and foil. Reheat by steaming or microwaving.

Enjoy your Tamales de Rajas con Queso, a delicious and satisfying dish perfect for any occasion!

**Mole Verde**

**Ingredients:**

**For the Mole Verde:**

- 1 lb (450g) tomatillos, husked and rinsed
- 2-3 green chiles (such as serrano, jalapeño, or poblano), stems removed
- 1 small onion, coarsely chopped
- 3 cloves garlic, peeled
- 1 cup fresh cilantro, chopped (stems and leaves)
- 1/2 cup fresh parsley, chopped (optional)
- 1/4 cup pumpkin seeds (pepitas), toasted
- 1/4 cup sesame seeds, toasted
- 1/2 cup chicken or vegetable broth (more as needed)
- 1 tablespoon vegetable oil
- 1/2 teaspoon ground cumin
- 1/2 teaspoon dried oregano
- 1/2 teaspoon ground coriander
- Salt and freshly ground black pepper, to taste

**For Garnishing (optional):**

- Crumbled queso fresco or cotija cheese
- Sliced radishes
- Fresh cilantro, chopped
- Lime wedges

**Instructions:**

1. **Prepare the Ingredients:**
   - **Roast the Tomatillos and Chiles:** Preheat your broiler or grill. Place the tomatillos and green chiles on a baking sheet. Roast under the broiler or on the grill, turning occasionally, until they are charred and softened, about 5-10 minutes. Alternatively, you can roast them in a dry skillet over medium heat.
   - **Toast the Seeds:** While the tomatillos and chiles are roasting, toast the pumpkin seeds and sesame seeds in a dry skillet over medium heat until golden and fragrant. Be careful not to burn them.
2. **Blend the Sauce:**
   - Once the tomatillos and chiles are roasted, transfer them to a blender or food processor. Add the coarsely chopped onion, garlic cloves, cilantro, and parsley (if using). Blend until smooth.
   - Add the toasted pumpkin seeds and sesame seeds to the blender. Blend again until the mixture is smooth and well combined.
3. **Cook the Mole Verde:**

- Heat the vegetable oil in a large skillet or saucepan over medium heat.
- Pour the blended mixture into the skillet and cook, stirring occasionally, for about 10 minutes. This helps to develop the flavors and thicken the sauce.
- Add the ground cumin, dried oregano, ground coriander, salt, and black pepper. Stir well to combine.
- Gradually add the chicken or vegetable broth, stirring constantly, until you reach your desired consistency. The sauce should be smooth and pourable but not too thin. Simmer for an additional 10-15 minutes, allowing the flavors to meld and the sauce to thicken.

4. **Adjust Seasoning:**
   - Taste the mole verde and adjust the seasoning with additional salt, pepper, or more lime juice if needed.
5. **Serve:**
   - Mole Verde can be served over grilled or roasted chicken, pork, or even vegetables. It's also excellent as a topping for tacos, enchiladas, or tamales.
   - Garnish with crumbled queso fresco or cotija cheese, sliced radishes, fresh cilantro, and lime wedges, if desired.

**Tips:**

- **Heat Level:** Adjust the number and type of green chiles based on your heat preference. Serrano chiles will add more heat compared to jalapeños.
- **Consistency:** If the sauce becomes too thick, you can thin it out with additional chicken or vegetable broth.
- **Make-Ahead:** Mole Verde can be made ahead of time and stored in the refrigerator for up to a week. It also freezes well for up to 3 months.

Enjoy your Mole Verde, a fresh and zesty sauce that brings a burst of flavor to any dish!

**Tinga de Pollo**

**Ingredients:**

**For the Chicken:**

- 3-4 boneless, skinless chicken breasts or thighs (about 1.5 lbs/700g)
- 1 bay leaf
- 1 onion, halved
- 2 cloves garlic
- 1 teaspoon salt
- Water (enough to cover the chicken)

**For the Sauce:**

- 2 tablespoons vegetable oil
- 1 large onion, finely chopped
- 4 cloves garlic, minced
- 1 can (14.5 oz/410g) diced tomatoes, or 3-4 medium ripe tomatoes, peeled and chopped
- 2-3 chipotle chiles in adobo sauce (canned)
- 1 tablespoon adobo sauce (from the chipotle can)
- 1 teaspoon dried oregano
- 1 teaspoon ground cumin
- 1 teaspoon smoked paprika (optional, for extra smokiness)
- 1/2 cup chicken broth (more if needed)
- Salt and freshly ground black pepper, to taste

**For Serving:**

- Corn or flour tortillas
- Shredded lettuce
- Sliced radishes
- Sliced avocado
- Crumbled queso fresco
- Fresh cilantro, chopped
- Lime wedges

**Instructions:**

1. **Cook the Chicken:**
    - Place the chicken breasts or thighs in a large pot. Add the bay leaf, onion, garlic, salt, and enough water to cover the chicken.
    - Bring to a boil, then reduce the heat to low and simmer for about 20-25 minutes, or until the chicken is cooked through and easily shreds with a fork.
    - Remove the chicken from the pot and let it cool slightly. Reserve the broth. Shred the chicken using two forks or your hands.

2. **Prepare the Sauce:**
    - In a large skillet, heat the vegetable oil over medium heat.
    - Add the finely chopped onion and cook until softened and translucent, about 5 minutes.
    - Stir in the minced garlic and cook for another minute.
    - Add the diced tomatoes (or chopped fresh tomatoes) and cook for 5-7 minutes, until the tomatoes break down and the mixture thickens slightly.
    - Blend the chipotle chiles with adobo sauce, oregano, cumin, and smoked paprika (if using) in a blender or food processor until smooth. Add a little of the tomato mixture if needed to help blend.
    - Pour the chipotle mixture into the skillet with the tomatoes and onion. Stir well to combine.
3. **Combine Chicken and Sauce:**
    - Add the shredded chicken to the skillet. Stir to coat the chicken with the sauce.
    - Pour in the chicken broth, a little at a time, until you reach your desired consistency. The sauce should be thick but not dry. Simmer for 10-15 minutes, allowing the flavors to meld and the sauce to thicken further. Adjust seasoning with salt and black pepper to taste.
4. **Serve:**
    - Serve the Tinga de Pollo hot over warm corn or flour tortillas. You can also use it as a filling for tacos, tostadas, or even as a topping for rice.
    - Garnish with shredded lettuce, sliced radishes, sliced avocado, crumbled queso fresco, and chopped fresh cilantro. Serve with lime wedges on the side.

## Tips:

- **Chipotle Chiles:** Adjust the number of chipotle chiles to control the heat level. The more chiles you add, the spicier the dish will be.
- **Tomato Options:** Using canned diced tomatoes is convenient, but fresh tomatoes can be used for a fresher taste. If using fresh tomatoes, peel and chop them before adding to the sauce.
- **Make-Ahead:** Tinga de Pollo can be made ahead of time and stored in the refrigerator for up to 4 days. It also freezes well for up to 3 months.

Enjoy your Tinga de Pollo, a richly flavored and versatile dish that's perfect for a quick weeknight meal or a special gathering!

**Sopes de Carne Asada**

**Ingredients:**

**For the Carne Asada:**

- 1.5 lbs (700g) flank steak or skirt steak
- 1/4 cup soy sauce
- 1/4 cup lime juice (about 2 limes)
- 3 cloves garlic, minced
- 1 tablespoon vegetable oil
- 1 teaspoon ground cumin
- 1 teaspoon dried oregano
- 1 teaspoon smoked paprika
- 1/2 teaspoon black pepper
- 1/2 teaspoon salt

**For the Sopes:**

- 2 cups masa harina (corn flour for tortillas)
- 1/2 teaspoon salt
- 1 cup warm water (more if needed)
- Vegetable oil (for frying)

**For Garnishing:**

- Refried beans (optional)
- Shredded lettuce
- Sliced radishes
- Crumbled queso fresco or cotija cheese
- Fresh cilantro, chopped
- Salsa or hot sauce
- Lime wedges

**Instructions:**

1. **Prepare the Carne Asada:**
   - **Marinate the Beef:** In a bowl, combine the soy sauce, lime juice, minced garlic, vegetable oil, ground cumin, dried oregano, smoked paprika, black pepper, and salt. Mix well.
   - Place the flank steak or skirt steak in a resealable plastic bag or shallow dish and pour the marinade over it. Seal the bag or cover the dish and refrigerate for at least 1 hour, preferably overnight.
   - **Grill the Beef:** Preheat a grill or grill pan to medium-high heat. Remove the steak from the marinade and grill for about 4-6 minutes per side, or until the desired level of doneness is achieved. Let the steak rest for a few minutes before slicing.
   - **Slice the Beef:** Thinly slice the grilled steak against the grain, then chop into small pieces.

2. **Prepare the Sopes:**
   - **Make the Dough:** In a large bowl, mix the masa harina and salt. Gradually add warm water, mixing with your hands, until a soft and pliable dough forms. The dough should be moist but not sticky.
   - **Form the Sopes:** Divide the dough into 8-10 equal portions. Roll each portion into a ball, then flatten into a disc about 1/4 inch thick. Use your fingers to create a raised edge around the perimeter of each disc to form a small, thick tortilla with a border.
   - **Cook the Sopes:** Heat a skillet or griddle over medium heat. Cook each sope for about 1-2 minutes on each side, until lightly browned and cooked through. Keep warm.
   - **Fry the Sopes (optional):** For a crisper texture, heat vegetable oil in a skillet over medium heat. Fry each sope for about 30 seconds to 1 minute on each side, or until golden brown. Drain on paper towels.
3. **Assemble the Sopes:**
   - **Spread Refried Beans (Optional):** If using refried beans, spread a thin layer on each sope.
   - **Add Carne Asada:** Top each sope with a portion of the chopped carne asada.
   - **Garnish:** Add shredded lettuce, sliced radishes, crumbled queso fresco, and fresh cilantro. Drizzle with salsa or hot sauce to taste.
   - **Serve:** Serve with lime wedges on the side for a burst of freshness.

**Tips:**

- **Masa Consistency:** The masa dough should be soft and easy to work with. If it's too dry, add a little more water; if too sticky, add a bit more masa harina.
- **Carne Asada Alternative:** If you don't have access to a grill, you can cook the steak in a skillet or under a broiler. Adjust cooking times based on the thickness of the steak.
- **Make-Ahead:** The carne asada can be cooked ahead of time and stored in the refrigerator for up to 3 days. Reheat before assembling the sopes.

Enjoy your Sopes de Carne Asada, a delightful and satisfying dish that brings a taste of Mexican street food to your table!

**Pescado a la Veracruzana**

**Ingredients:**

**For the Fish:**

- 4 boneless, skinless fish fillets (such as tilapia, snapper, or cod)
- Salt and freshly ground black pepper, to taste
- 1 tablespoon vegetable oil (for searing)

**For the Veracruzana Sauce:**

- 2 tablespoons vegetable oil
- 1 onion, finely chopped
- 3 cloves garlic, minced
- 1 can (14.5 oz/410g) diced tomatoes (or 4-5 fresh tomatoes, peeled and chopped)
- 1/2 cup green olives, pitted and sliced
- 1/4 cup capers, drained
- 1/2 cup white wine (optional, or use chicken broth)
- 1/2 teaspoon dried oregano
- 1/2 teaspoon ground cumin
- 1/4 teaspoon ground paprika
- 1/4 teaspoon red pepper flakes (optional, for extra heat)
- 1 bay leaf
- 1 tablespoon fresh lime juice (or to taste)
- Salt and freshly ground black pepper, to taste

**For Garnishing:**

- Fresh cilantro, chopped
- Lime wedges

**Instructions:**

1. **Prepare the Fish:**
   - Season the fish fillets with salt and black pepper on both sides.
   - Heat vegetable oil in a large skillet over medium-high heat. Sear the fish fillets for 2-3 minutes per side, or until they are golden brown and cooked through. Remove the fish from the skillet and set aside. (The fish will finish cooking in the sauce.)
2. **Prepare the Veracruzana Sauce:**
   - In the same skillet, add 2 tablespoons of vegetable oil and heat over medium heat.
   - Add the finely chopped onion and cook until softened and translucent, about 5 minutes.
   - Stir in the minced garlic and cook for another minute.
   - Add the diced tomatoes (or chopped fresh tomatoes) and cook for 5-7 minutes, until the tomatoes break down and the mixture starts to thicken.

- Stir in the green olives, capers, white wine (or chicken broth), dried oregano, ground cumin, paprika, red pepper flakes (if using), and bay leaf. Simmer for another 5-7 minutes, allowing the flavors to meld together.
    - Add the fresh lime juice and season the sauce with salt and black pepper to taste.
3. **Combine Fish and Sauce:**
    - Gently return the seared fish fillets to the skillet, placing them into the simmering sauce. Spoon some sauce over the fish to coat.
    - Simmer for 5-10 minutes, or until the fish is fully cooked and has absorbed the flavors of the sauce. Be careful not to overcook the fish.
4. **Serve:**
    - Garnish with chopped fresh cilantro and serve with lime wedges on the side.
    - Pescado a la Veracruzana is delicious served over rice, with warm tortillas, or alongside a fresh salad.

**Tips:**

- **Fish Choices:** While tilapia, snapper, or cod are commonly used, you can use any firm white fish of your choice.
- **Tomato Sauce:** If using fresh tomatoes, make sure to peel them before chopping. You can also use canned tomato sauce or crushed tomatoes for a smoother sauce.
- **Wine:** The white wine adds depth to the sauce, but you can substitute with more chicken broth if preferred.

Enjoy your Pescado a la Veracruzana, a dish that beautifully showcases the vibrant and fresh flavors of Mexican cuisine!

**Chilaquiles Rojos**

**Ingredients:**

**For the Red Sauce:**

- 6-8 dried guajillo chiles
- 2-3 dried ancho chiles
- 1 medium onion, coarsely chopped
- 2 cloves garlic, peeled
- 2-3 medium tomatoes, chopped (or one 14.5 oz can of diced tomatoes)
- 1 cup chicken or vegetable broth
- 1 tablespoon vegetable oil
- 1 teaspoon dried oregano
- 1/2 teaspoon ground cumin
- Salt and freshly ground black pepper, to taste

**For the Chilaquiles:**

- 10-12 corn tortillas
- Vegetable oil (for frying)
- 2 cups shredded chicken (optional)
- 1/2 cup crumbled queso fresco or cotija cheese
- 1/2 cup sour cream or Mexican crema (optional)
- 2-3 green onions, thinly sliced
- 1/4 cup fresh cilantro, chopped
- 1 lime, cut into wedges

**For Garnishing (optional):**

- Sliced radishes
- Sliced avocado
- Fried or poached eggs
- Salsa verde (for additional flavor)

**Instructions:**

1. **Prepare the Red Sauce:**
    - **Toast the Chiles:** Heat a dry skillet over medium heat. Toast the dried guajillo and ancho chiles for about 30 seconds on each side, until fragrant. Be careful not to burn them.
    - **Soak the Chiles:** Place the toasted chiles in a bowl and cover with hot water. Let them soak for about 15 minutes, until softened.
    - **Blend the Sauce:** Drain the chiles and transfer them to a blender. Add the chopped onion, garlic, tomatoes, and chicken or vegetable broth. Blend until smooth.
    - **Cook the Sauce:** Heat the vegetable oil in a saucepan over medium heat. Add the blended sauce and cook for about 10-15 minutes, stirring occasionally, until

the sauce thickens and darkens in color. Stir in the dried oregano, ground cumin, salt, and black pepper. Adjust seasoning to taste.
2. **Prepare the Tortilla Chips:**
    - **Cut the Tortillas:** Cut the corn tortillas into triangles or strips.
    - **Fry the Chips:** Heat vegetable oil in a large skillet or deep fryer over medium-high heat. Fry the tortilla pieces in batches until crispy and golden brown. Drain on paper towels and season with a little salt while still hot.
3. **Assemble the Chilaquiles:**
    - **Combine Chips and Sauce:** In a large skillet, heat a bit of vegetable oil over medium heat. Add the fried tortilla chips and pour the red sauce over them. Toss gently to coat the chips evenly with the sauce. Cook for about 2-3 minutes, just long enough for the chips to absorb some of the sauce but still remain crisp.
4. **Add Optional Ingredients:**
    - If using shredded chicken, sprinkle it over the chilaquiles before serving.
    - Top with crumbled queso fresco or cotija cheese, sour cream or Mexican crema (if using), sliced green onions, and fresh cilantro.
5. **Serve:**
    - Serve the chilaquiles hot, garnished with additional toppings such as sliced radishes, avocado slices, and fried or poached eggs if desired.
    - Provide lime wedges on the side for an extra burst of freshness. Salsa verde can be served on the side for additional flavor.

**Tips:**

- **Chili Options:** Adjust the type and amount of dried chiles based on your heat preference. Guajillo chiles add a mild, smoky flavor, while ancho chiles are slightly sweeter.
- **Crispiness:** To keep the tortilla chips crispy, don't let them sit in the sauce too long. If you prefer softer chilaquiles, allow them to simmer a bit longer in the sauce.
- **Make-Ahead:** The red sauce can be made ahead of time and stored in the refrigerator for up to a week or frozen for up to 3 months. Just reheat and toss with fresh tortilla chips before serving.

Enjoy your Chilaquiles Rojos, a flavorful and comforting dish that's perfect for starting your day off right!

**Arroz con Pollo**

**Ingredients:**

**For the Dish:**

- 4 bone-in, skinless chicken thighs (or a mix of thighs and drumsticks)
- Salt and freshly ground black pepper, to taste
- 1 tablespoon vegetable oil
- 1 onion, finely chopped
- 1 bell pepper (red or green), chopped
- 2 cloves garlic, minced
- 1 cup long-grain rice
- 1 can (14.5 oz/410g) diced tomatoes (or 2 medium tomatoes, chopped)
- 1 cup frozen peas (or fresh peas if available)
- 1/2 cup pitted green olives, sliced (optional)
- 1/4 cup capers (optional)
- 1 cup chicken broth
- 1/2 cup dry white wine (optional)
- 1 teaspoon ground cumin
- 1 teaspoon paprika
- 1/2 teaspoon dried oregano
- 1/2 teaspoon turmeric or saffron (for color, optional)
- 1 bay leaf

**For Garnishing:**

- Fresh cilantro, chopped
- Lemon or lime wedges

**Instructions:**

1. **Prepare the Chicken:**
   - Season the chicken pieces with salt and black pepper.
   - Heat the vegetable oil in a large skillet or Dutch oven over medium-high heat. Add the chicken pieces and brown on all sides, about 5-7 minutes. Remove the chicken and set aside.
2. **Cook the Vegetables:**
   - In the same skillet, add the chopped onion and bell pepper. Cook until softened, about 5 minutes.
   - Stir in the minced garlic and cook for another minute.
3. **Prepare the Rice:**
   - Add the rice to the skillet and cook, stirring frequently, until the rice is lightly toasted, about 2-3 minutes.
   - Stir in the diced tomatoes (with their juices), chicken broth, white wine (if using), ground cumin, paprika, dried oregano, turmeric or saffron (if using), and bay leaf.
4. **Combine Ingredients:**
   - Return the browned chicken pieces to the skillet, nestling them into the rice mixture.

- Bring to a boil, then reduce the heat to low and cover the skillet. Simmer for about 20-25 minutes, or until the rice is tender and the chicken is cooked through.
5. **Add Peas and Optional Ingredients:**
    - About 5 minutes before the cooking time is up, stir in the frozen peas, sliced green olives, and capers (if using). Adjust the seasoning with salt and black pepper as needed.
6. **Finish and Serve:**
    - Once the rice is cooked and the liquid is absorbed, remove the bay leaf and discard.
    - Garnish with chopped fresh cilantro and serve with lemon or lime wedges on the side.

**Tips:**

- **Rice:** Long-grain rice works best for this dish as it stays fluffy and separates well. You can also use Basmati rice if preferred.
- **Saffron:** If using saffron, dissolve it in a small amount of warm water before adding it to the dish. It adds a unique flavor and color but can be omitted if unavailable.
- **Vegetables:** Feel free to add other vegetables like carrots or green beans based on your preference or what you have on hand.

Enjoy your Arroz con Pollo, a hearty and flavorful dish that brings together tender chicken and perfectly seasoned rice in one delicious pot!

**Flautas de Pollo**

**Ingredients:**

**For the Chicken Filling:**

- 2 cups cooked, shredded chicken (about 2-3 chicken breasts or thighs)
- 1 tablespoon vegetable oil
- 1 onion, finely chopped
- 2 cloves garlic, minced
- 1 cup chicken broth
- 1 teaspoon ground cumin
- 1 teaspoon paprika
- 1/2 teaspoon dried oregano
- 1/2 teaspoon chili powder
- Salt and freshly ground black pepper, to taste

**For the Flautas:**

- 10-12 small corn tortillas (or flour tortillas if preferred)
- Vegetable oil (for frying)

**For Garnishing:**

- Shredded lettuce
- Crumbled queso fresco or cotija cheese
- Sour cream or Mexican crema
- Salsa or hot sauce
- Sliced avocado
- Fresh cilantro, chopped
- Lime wedges

**Instructions:**

1. **Prepare the Chicken Filling:**
   - **Cook the Aromatics:** Heat vegetable oil in a skillet over medium heat. Add the finely chopped onion and cook until softened and translucent, about 5 minutes.
   - **Add Garlic:** Stir in the minced garlic and cook for another minute.
   - **Add Chicken and Spices:** Add the shredded chicken to the skillet, followed by the chicken broth, ground cumin, paprika, dried oregano, chili powder, salt, and black pepper.
   - **Simmer:** Cook the mixture over medium heat for about 5-7 minutes, or until the liquid has reduced and the chicken is well coated with the spices. Adjust seasoning to taste. Remove from heat and let it cool slightly.
2. **Assemble the Flautas:**
   - **Warm Tortillas:** To make rolling easier, warm the tortillas in a dry skillet over medium heat for about 20-30 seconds on each side until pliable. Alternatively, wrap them in a damp paper towel and microwave for 30-45 seconds.

      - **Fill the Tortillas:** Place a small amount of the chicken filling in the center of each tortilla. Roll the tortilla tightly around the filling and secure with a toothpick if needed.
3. **Fry the Flautas:**
      - **Heat Oil:** Heat vegetable oil in a large skillet or deep fryer over medium-high heat. The oil should be hot but not smoking.
      - **Fry the Flautas:** Fry the flautas in batches, turning occasionally, until they are golden brown and crispy on all sides, about 3-4 minutes. Be sure not to overcrowd the skillet.
      - **Drain:** Remove the flautas from the oil and drain on paper towels.
4. **Serve:**
      - **Garnish:** Arrange the hot flautas on a serving platter. Top with shredded lettuce, crumbled cheese, a dollop of sour cream or Mexican crema, and your favorite salsa or hot sauce.
      - **Add Extras:** Garnish with sliced avocado, fresh cilantro, and lime wedges.

**Tips:**

- **Chicken Filling:** You can use leftover rotisserie chicken or cook chicken specifically for this dish. Shredded chicken breast or thighs work well.
- **Tortilla Options:** While corn tortillas are traditional, flour tortillas can be used if preferred. Flour tortillas may be easier to roll but will result in a slightly different texture.
- **Make-Ahead:** The chicken filling can be made ahead of time and stored in the refrigerator for up to 3 days. Assemble and fry the flautas just before serving.

Enjoy your Flautas de Pollo, crispy and flavorful rolls filled with delicious chicken, and perfect for any occasion!

**Huachinango a la Veracruza**

**Ingredients:**

**For the Fish:**

- 1 whole red snapper (about 2-3 pounds), cleaned and scaled (or 4-6 fillets if preferred)
- Salt and freshly ground black pepper, to taste
- 1 tablespoon vegetable oil (for searing)

**For the Veracruzana Sauce:**

- 2 tablespoons vegetable oil
- 1 onion, finely chopped
- 3 cloves garlic, minced
- 1 can (14.5 oz/410g) diced tomatoes (or 4-5 fresh tomatoes, peeled and chopped)
- 1/2 cup green olives, pitted and sliced
- 1/4 cup capers, drained
- 1/2 cup white wine (optional, or use chicken broth)
- 1/2 teaspoon dried oregano
- 1/2 teaspoon ground cumin
- 1/4 teaspoon smoked paprika
- 1/4 teaspoon red pepper flakes (optional, for extra heat)
- 1 bay leaf
- 1 tablespoon fresh lime juice (or to taste)
- Salt and freshly ground black pepper, to taste

**For Garnishing:**

- Fresh cilantro, chopped
- Lime wedges

**Instructions:**

1. **Prepare the Fish:**
   - **Season the Fish:** Season the red snapper (or fillets) with salt and black pepper on both sides.
   - **Sear the Fish:** Heat vegetable oil in a large skillet or Dutch oven over medium-high heat. Add the whole fish or fillets and sear for 2-3 minutes per side, until lightly browned. Remove the fish and set aside.
2. **Prepare the Veracruzana Sauce:**
   - **Cook the Aromatics:** In the same skillet, add 2 tablespoons of vegetable oil and heat over medium heat. Add the finely chopped onion and cook until softened and translucent, about 5 minutes.
   - **Add Garlic:** Stir in the minced garlic and cook for another minute.
   - **Add Tomatoes:** Add the diced tomatoes (or chopped fresh tomatoes) to the skillet and cook for 5-7 minutes, until the tomatoes break down and the mixture starts to thicken.

- **Add Other Ingredients:** Stir in the sliced green olives, capers, white wine (or chicken broth), dried oregano, ground cumin, smoked paprika, red pepper flakes (if using), and bay leaf. Simmer for 5-7 minutes, allowing the flavors to meld together.
- **Add Lime Juice:** Stir in the fresh lime juice and season the sauce with salt and black pepper to taste.
3. **Combine Fish and Sauce:**
    - **Return the Fish:** Gently return the seared fish to the skillet, placing it into the simmering sauce. Spoon some sauce over the fish to coat.
    - **Simmer:** Simmer for about 10-15 minutes, or until the fish is fully cooked and has absorbed the flavors of the sauce. Be careful not to overcook the fish.
4. **Serve:**
    - **Garnish:** Garnish with chopped fresh cilantro and serve with lime wedges on the side.
    - **Accompaniments:** Huachinango a la Veracruzana is typically served with rice, warm tortillas, or a fresh salad.

**Tips:**

- **Fish Selection:** Red snapper is traditional, but you can use other firm white fish if preferred. Make sure the fish is fresh for the best flavor.
- **Tomato Sauce:** If using fresh tomatoes, peel them before chopping. Canned diced tomatoes work well for a quicker preparation.
- **Wine Substitute:** The white wine adds depth to the sauce, but you can substitute it with more chicken broth if preferred.

Enjoy your Huachinango a la Veracruzana, a flavorful and vibrant dish that showcases the fresh, coastal flavors of Veracruz!

**Gorditas de Chicharrón Prensado**

**Ingredients:**

**For the Gorditas:**

- 2 cups masa harina (corn flour for tortillas)
- 1 1/2 cups warm water (more if needed)
- 1/2 teaspoon baking powder
- 1/2 teaspoon salt

**For the Chicharrón Prensado Filling:**

- 1 pound chicharrón prensado (pressed pork cracklings)
- 1 tablespoon vegetable oil
- 1 small onion, finely chopped
- 2 cloves garlic, minced
- 1/2 cup chicken broth (or water)
- 1/2 teaspoon ground cumin
- 1/2 teaspoon dried oregano
- 1/4 teaspoon chili powder (optional, for a bit of heat)
- Salt and freshly ground black pepper, to taste

**For Serving (optional):**

- Salsa verde or roja
- Sour cream or Mexican crema
- Shredded lettuce or cabbage
- Sliced radishes
- Fresh cilantro, chopped
- Lime wedges

**Instructions:**

1. **Prepare the Chicharrón Prensado Filling:**
    - **Heat Oil:** In a skillet, heat the vegetable oil over medium heat.
    - **Cook Aromatics:** Add the finely chopped onion and cook until softened and translucent, about 5 minutes.
    - **Add Garlic:** Stir in the minced garlic and cook for another minute.
    - **Add Chicharrón:** Crumble the chicharrón prensado into the skillet. Stir and cook for a few minutes.
    - **Add Broth and Spices:** Pour in the chicken broth (or water), and stir in the ground cumin, dried oregano, chili powder (if using), salt, and black pepper.
    - **Simmer:** Cook the mixture, stirring occasionally, until the liquid is mostly absorbed and the chicharrón is well seasoned and tender. Adjust seasoning to taste. Remove from heat and let it cool slightly.
2. **Prepare the Gorditas:**

- **Mix Masa:** In a large bowl, combine the masa harina, baking powder, and salt. Gradually add warm water, mixing with your hands until a soft, pliable dough forms. The dough should be moist but not sticky.
- **Shape Gorditas:** Divide the dough into 10-12 equal pieces. Flatten each piece into a thick disc, about 1/2 inch thick, using your hands or a tortilla press.
- **Cook Gorditas:** Heat a griddle or non-stick skillet over medium-high heat. Cook the gorditas for about 2-3 minutes on each side, or until they develop golden brown spots and are cooked through. You may need to press them lightly with a spatula to ensure they cook evenly.

3. **Assemble the Gorditas:**
   - **Cut and Stuff:** Once the gorditas are cooked, slice them open on one side to create a pocket. Spoon the chicharrón prensado filling into the pocket.
4. **Serve:**
   - **Add Toppings:** Serve the stuffed gorditas with optional toppings such as salsa verde or roja, sour cream or Mexican crema, shredded lettuce or cabbage, sliced radishes, chopped cilantro, and lime wedges.

**Tips:**

- **Chicharrón Prensado:** If you can't find chicharrón prensado, you can use regular chicharrón (pork cracklings) and chop it finely. You may need to add a bit more broth or water to make it easier to work with.
- **Dough Consistency:** If the masa dough feels too dry, add a bit more water, one tablespoon at a time. If too wet, add a little more masa harina.
- **Serving:** Gorditas de Chicharrón Prensado are great for a casual meal and can be served with a variety of sides and salsas. They are also delicious on their own!

Enjoy your Gorditas de Chicharrón Prensado, a delicious and satisfying Mexican treat that combines savory chicharrón with soft, homemade tortillas!

**Tostadas de Atún**

**Ingredients:**

**For the Tuna Topping:**

- 2 cans (5 oz each) tuna in olive oil or water, drained
- 1/4 cup mayonnaise
- 1 tablespoon sour cream or Mexican crema (optional)
- 1 tablespoon lime juice
- 1/4 cup red onion, finely chopped
- 1/4 cup fresh cilantro, chopped
- 1 small tomato, diced
- 1 jalapeño pepper, seeded and finely chopped (optional, for heat)
- Salt and freshly ground black pepper, to taste

**For the Tostadas:**

- 8-10 tostada shells (store-bought or homemade)
- 1 cup shredded lettuce or cabbage
- 1 avocado, sliced
- 1/4 cup crumbled queso fresco or cotija cheese (optional)
- Salsa or hot sauce (optional)

**For Garnishing:**

- Fresh cilantro, chopped
- Lime wedges
- Sliced radishes (optional)

**Instructions:**

1. **Prepare the Tuna Topping:**
    - **Combine Ingredients:** In a medium bowl, combine the drained tuna, mayonnaise, sour cream or Mexican crema (if using), lime juice, finely chopped red onion, fresh cilantro, diced tomato, and chopped jalapeño (if using).
    - **Season:** Mix well and season with salt and freshly ground black pepper to taste. Adjust the amount of lime juice and seasoning according to your preference. Refrigerate the tuna mixture until ready to use.
2. **Prepare the Tostadas:**
    - **Warm or Toast:** If using store-bought tostada shells, you can warm them in the oven for a few minutes to make them more crispy, or toast them on a skillet for extra crunch. If making homemade tostadas, bake or fry them until crisp.
3. **Assemble the Tostadas:**
    - **Layer Ingredients:** On each tostada shell, spread a layer of shredded lettuce or cabbage. Top with a generous spoonful of the tuna mixture.
    - **Add Toppings:** Garnish with slices of avocado, crumbled queso fresco or cotija cheese (if using), and a drizzle of salsa or hot sauce if desired.

4. **Serve:**
   - **Garnish:** Sprinkle with additional chopped cilantro and serve with lime wedges on the side for an extra burst of flavor.
   - **Optional:** Add sliced radishes for extra crunch and color.

**Tips:**

- **Tuna:** For the best flavor, use high-quality tuna in olive oil or water. You can also use fresh tuna or substitute with canned salmon if preferred.
- **Customization:** Feel free to customize the topping by adding ingredients like black beans, corn, or diced bell peppers to the tuna mixture.
- **Heat Level:** Adjust the amount of jalapeño and hot sauce to suit your preferred level of spiciness.

Enjoy your Tostadas de Atún, a refreshing and tasty dish that combines crispy tortillas with a zesty tuna topping!

**Camarones al Ajillo**

**Ingredients:**

- 1 pound large shrimp, peeled and deveined (tails on or off as desired)
- 1/4 cup olive oil
- 6-8 cloves garlic, thinly sliced
- 1/4 teaspoon red pepper flakes (adjust to taste for spiciness)
- 1/2 teaspoon smoked paprika (or regular paprika)
- 1/2 teaspoon dried oregano
- 1/4 cup white wine (optional, or use chicken broth)
- 2 tablespoons fresh lemon juice (or lime juice)
- Salt and freshly ground black pepper, to taste
- Fresh parsley, chopped (for garnish)
- Lemon or lime wedges (for serving)

**Instructions:**

1. **Prepare the Shrimp:**
   - **Season:** Pat the shrimp dry with paper towels and season with salt and black pepper.
2. **Cook the Garlic:**
   - **Heat Oil:** In a large skillet, heat the olive oil over medium heat.
   - **Add Garlic:** Add the sliced garlic to the skillet and cook, stirring frequently, until the garlic is golden brown and fragrant, about 2-3 minutes. Be careful not to let the garlic burn, as it can become bitter.
3. **Add Shrimp:**
   - **Cook Shrimp:** Increase the heat to medium-high and add the seasoned shrimp to the skillet. Cook for 2-3 minutes on each side, or until the shrimp are pink and opaque.
4. **Add Flavorings:**
   - **Add Spices:** Stir in the red pepper flakes, smoked paprika, and dried oregano.
   - **Deglaze:** If using white wine, pour it into the skillet and scrape up any browned bits from the bottom of the pan. Let it simmer for 1-2 minutes until the wine is reduced slightly. If not using wine, just skip this step and proceed.
   - **Add Lemon Juice:** Stir in the fresh lemon juice and adjust seasoning with additional salt and pepper if needed.
5. **Finish and Serve:**
   - **Garnish:** Sprinkle the cooked shrimp with chopped fresh parsley.
   - **Serve:** Serve the Camarones al Ajillo with lemon or lime wedges on the side. This dish pairs wonderfully with crusty bread, rice, or pasta to soak up the flavorful sauce.

**Tips:**

- **Garlic:** Thinly slicing the garlic helps to infuse more flavor into the oil. If you prefer a milder garlic flavor, you can mince the garlic instead.
- **Shrimp Size:** Large shrimp work best for this dish, but you can use any size shrimp you prefer. Just adjust the cooking time accordingly.

- **Wine Substitute:** If you don't have white wine, you can use chicken broth or just skip this step and continue with the recipe.

Enjoy your Camarones al Ajillo, a delicious and aromatic shrimp dish that's sure to impress with its rich garlic flavor and simplicity!

**Cactus Salad (Nopales)**

**Ingredients:**

**For the Salad:**

- 4-5 cactus pads (nopales), cleaned and trimmed
- 1/4 cup red onion, finely chopped
- 1 medium tomato, diced
- 1 avocado, diced
- 1/4 cup fresh cilantro, chopped
- 1-2 serrano or jalapeño peppers, finely chopped (optional, for heat)
- 1/2 cup crumbled queso fresco or cotija cheese (optional)
- Salt and freshly ground black pepper, to taste

**For the Dressing:**

- 1/4 cup olive oil
- 2 tablespoons fresh lime juice (or lemon juice)
- 1 tablespoon apple cider vinegar or white wine vinegar
- 1 teaspoon honey or agave syrup (optional, for a touch of sweetness)
- 1 clove garlic, minced
- 1/2 teaspoon ground cumin
- 1/2 teaspoon dried oregano
- Salt and freshly ground black pepper, to taste

**Instructions:**

1. **Prepare the Nopales:**
   - **Clean and Trim:** Use a vegetable peeler or a knife to remove the thorns from the cactus pads. Rinse them well under cold water.
   - **Cook:** Bring a large pot of water to a boil and add a pinch of salt. Add the cactus pads and cook for about 10-15 minutes, or until tender and slightly translucent. Stir occasionally.
   - **Cool and Chop:** Drain the cooked nopales and let them cool slightly. Cut them into thin strips or bite-sized pieces.
2. **Prepare the Salad:**
   - **Combine Ingredients:** In a large bowl, combine the chopped cactus, red onion, diced tomato, diced avocado, chopped cilantro, and chopped serrano or jalapeño peppers (if using). Gently toss to mix.
3. **Prepare the Dressing:**
   - **Mix Dressing:** In a small bowl or jar, whisk together the olive oil, fresh lime juice, apple cider vinegar, honey or agave syrup (if using), minced garlic, ground cumin, dried oregano, salt, and black pepper.
4. **Dress the Salad:**
   - **Toss:** Pour the dressing over the cactus mixture and toss gently to coat all the ingredients evenly.
5. **Serve:**
   - **Garnish:** If desired, sprinkle crumbled queso fresco or cotija cheese on top.

- **Enjoy:** Serve the cactus salad immediately, or chill it in the refrigerator for about 30 minutes to let the flavors meld together.

**Tips:**

- **Nopales:** Fresh cactus pads can be found in Latin American or specialty grocery stores. You can also use canned or jarred nopales if fresh ones are not available; just rinse and drain them before using.
- **Texture:** Cook the nopales until they are tender but still slightly crisp. Overcooking can make them slimy.
- **Heat Level:** Adjust the amount of serrano or jalapeño peppers according to your heat preference. You can omit them if you prefer a milder salad.

Enjoy your Cactus Salad (Nopales), a vibrant and healthy dish that's packed with flavor and perfect for a light meal or a refreshing side!

**Chiles Rellenos de Queso**

**Ingredients:**

**For the Chiles:**

- 6 large poblano peppers
- 2 cups shredded cheese (such as Monterey Jack, Oaxaca, or a blend of cheeses)
- 1/2 cup all-purpose flour (for dusting)

**For the Batter:**

- 3 large eggs
- 1/2 cup all-purpose flour
- 1/2 teaspoon baking powder
- 1/4 teaspoon salt
- 1/4 teaspoon ground black pepper

**For Frying:**

- Vegetable oil (for frying)

**For Garnishing (optional):**

- Salsa roja or salsa verde
- Fresh cilantro, chopped
- Sour cream or Mexican crema

**Instructions:**

1. **Prepare the Peppers:**
   - **Roast Peppers:** Place the poblano peppers on a baking sheet under the broiler, or directly over a gas flame. Roast them until the skin is blackened and blistered, turning occasionally to ensure even roasting. This should take about 5-10 minutes.
   - **Steam and Peel:** Transfer the roasted peppers to a paper bag or a covered bowl and let them steam for about 10 minutes. This helps loosen the skin. Once cool enough to handle, peel off the blackened skin, remove the stems, and carefully slit each pepper down one side to remove the seeds and membranes. Be gentle to keep the peppers intact.
2. **Stuff the Peppers:**
   - **Fill with Cheese:** Stuff each pepper with shredded cheese. If the peppers are very large, you might want to cut the cheese into strips or chunks to fit better.
3. **Prepare the Batter:**
   - **Separate Eggs:** Separate the egg yolks from the whites. Place the whites in a large mixing bowl and beat with an electric mixer until stiff peaks form.
   - **Mix Yolks and Flour:** In another bowl, whisk the egg yolks with 1/2 cup flour, baking powder, salt, and pepper until smooth.
   - **Fold Together:** Gently fold the egg yolk mixture into the beaten egg whites, being careful not to deflate the mixture too much.

4. **Fry the Peppers:**
   - **Heat Oil:** Heat about 1-2 inches of vegetable oil in a large skillet or deep fryer over medium-high heat until hot (about 350°F or 175°C).
   - **Coat and Fry:** Lightly dust each stuffed pepper with flour to help the batter adhere. Dip the peppers into the batter, coating them evenly. Carefully place them in the hot oil and fry until golden brown and crispy, about 2-3 minutes per side. Fry in batches if necessary, to avoid overcrowding the pan.
   - **Drain:** Remove the peppers from the oil with a slotted spoon and drain on paper towels.
5. **Serve:**
   - **Garnish:** Serve the Chiles Rellenos de Queso with salsa roja or salsa verde, and garnish with fresh cilantro and a dollop of sour cream or Mexican crema if desired.

**Tips:**

- **Cheese Selection:** Choose cheeses that melt well. Oaxaca, Monterey Jack, or even a combination of cheeses work well.
- **Pepper Preparation:** Make sure to remove all seeds and membranes from the peppers to reduce the heat and make room for the cheese.
- **Batter Texture:** The batter should be light and airy. If it seems too thick, you can gently fold in a little more beaten egg white.

Enjoy your Chiles Rellenos de Queso, a deliciously comforting and flavorful dish that's sure to be a hit at any meal!

**Caldo de Res**

**Ingredients:**

**For the Soup:**

- 2 pounds beef shank, beef short ribs, or bone-in beef stew meat, cut into large chunks
- 1 onion, quartered
- 3 cloves garlic, minced
- 1 bay leaf
- 1 teaspoon dried oregano
- 1 teaspoon ground cumin
- 6 cups beef broth (or water, if you prefer)
- 2 large carrots, peeled and cut into chunks
- 2-3 potatoes, peeled and cut into chunks
- 2-3 zucchini, cut into chunks
- 1 cup corn kernels (fresh, frozen, or canned)
- 1 cup green beans, trimmed and cut into pieces
- 1-2 tomatoes, chopped (or 1 can diced tomatoes)
- 1-2 chayotes, peeled and cut into chunks (optional)
- 1-2 ears of corn, cut into 2-inch pieces (optional)

**For Garnishing:**

- Fresh cilantro, chopped
- Lime wedges
- Sliced radishes
- Diced avocado
- Tortillas or crusty bread

**Instructions:**

1. **Prepare the Beef:**
    - **Brown the Meat:** In a large pot or Dutch oven, heat a little oil over medium-high heat. Add the beef chunks and brown on all sides. This step adds depth of flavor to the broth.
    - **Add Aromatics:** Add the quartered onion, minced garlic, bay leaf, dried oregano, and ground cumin. Cook for a few minutes until the onion is softened and fragrant.
2. **Simmer the Soup:**
    - **Add Broth:** Pour in the beef broth (or water) and bring to a boil. Skim off any foam or impurities that rise to the surface.
    - **Reduce Heat:** Reduce the heat to low, cover, and let it simmer for about 1.5 to 2 hours, or until the beef is tender and cooked through.
3. **Add Vegetables:**
    - **Carrots and Potatoes:** Add the carrots, potatoes, and corn kernels to the pot. Continue to simmer for about 10-15 minutes.
    - **Zucchini and Green Beans:** Add the zucchini and green beans (and chayotes and corn on the cob, if using). Cook for an additional 10-15 minutes, or until all vegetables are tender.

- **Tomatoes:** Stir in the chopped tomatoes or canned diced tomatoes. Cook for a few more minutes.
4. **Season and Adjust:**
    - **Taste and Adjust:** Taste the soup and adjust seasoning with salt and pepper as needed. You can also add more spices or herbs to suit your taste.
5. **Serve:**
    - **Garnish:** Serve the Caldo de Res hot, garnished with chopped fresh cilantro. Accompany with lime wedges, sliced radishes, diced avocado, and warm tortillas or crusty bread on the side.

**Tips:**

- **Meat:** For extra flavor, you can use a mix of beef cuts including bones with marrow. The marrow adds richness to the broth.
- **Vegetables:** Feel free to customize the vegetables based on what's in season or what you have on hand. Other vegetables like celery, bell peppers, or squash can be added.
- **Spice Level:** Adjust the seasoning to your liking. For a bit of heat, you can add sliced jalapeños or a pinch of red pepper flakes.

Enjoy your Caldo de Res, a deliciously warming and hearty soup that embodies the comfort and richness of traditional Mexican cooking!

**Pambazos**

## Ingredients:

- 3 1/2 cups all-purpose flour

- 1 tablespoon sugar
- 1 tablespoon salt
- 1 tablespoon instant yeast
- 1 1/4 cups warm water (110°F or 45°C)
- 2 tablespoons olive oil (optional, for extra softness)

## Instructions:

1. **Activate Yeast:**
    - In a small bowl, combine the warm water with the sugar. Sprinkle the instant yeast over the top and let it sit for about 5-10 minutes until it becomes frothy.
2. **Prepare Dough:**
    - In a large mixing bowl, whisk together the flour and salt. Make a well in the center and pour in the activated yeast mixture (and olive oil if using).
    - Mix until a dough starts to form. You can use a spoon or your hands for this.
3. **Knead Dough:**
    - Transfer the dough to a lightly floured surface and knead for about 8-10 minutes until it becomes smooth and elastic. You can also use a stand mixer with a dough hook if you have one.
4. **First Rise:**
    - Place the kneaded dough in a lightly oiled bowl, cover it with a damp cloth or plastic wrap, and let it rise in a warm, draft-free place for about 1 hour, or until it has doubled in size.
5. **Shape and Second Rise:**
    - Punch down the dough to release the air. Divide it into 8 equal pieces (or more if you prefer smaller rolls).
    - Shape each piece into a ball and place them on a baking sheet lined with parchment paper. Flatten each ball slightly to form the desired shape (oval or round).
    - Cover the shaped dough with a cloth and let it rise again for about 30 minutes.
6. **Preheat Oven:**
    - Preheat your oven to 375°F (190°C).
7. **Bake:**
    - Bake the rolls in the preheated oven for about 20-25 minutes, or until they are golden brown and sound hollow when tapped on the bottom.
8. **Cool:**
    - Let the bread cool on a wire rack before using.

This recipe will give you a crusty, soft roll that's perfect for pambazos or other sandwiches. Enjoy making and filling your pambazos!

**Huaraches de Carne Asada**

**Ingredients**

**For the Huaraches:**

- 2 cups masa harina (corn flour for tortillas)
- 1 1/2 cups warm water (more if needed)
- 1/2 teaspoon salt
- 1 tablespoon vegetable oil (optional, for a softer dough)

**For the Carne Asada:**

- 1 lb (450 g) beef skirt steak or flank steak
- 3 tablespoons olive oil
- 3 cloves garlic, minced
- 1 tablespoon lime juice
- 1 tablespoon soy sauce
- 1 tablespoon chili powder
- 1 teaspoon ground cumin
- 1 teaspoon paprika
- 1/2 teaspoon ground black pepper
- 1/2 teaspoon salt

**For Toppings:**

- Shredded lettuce or cabbage
- Diced tomatoes
- Sliced onions
- Chopped cilantro
- Crumbled queso fresco or shredded cheese
- Sour cream or Mexican crema
- Salsa or hot sauce

## Instructions

### 1. Prepare the Carne Asada:

1. **Marinate the Beef:**
    - In a bowl, combine olive oil, minced garlic, lime juice, soy sauce, chili powder, cumin, paprika, black pepper, and salt. Mix well.
    - Add the steak to the marinade, making sure it's evenly coated. Cover and refrigerate for at least 1 hour, or overnight for best results.
2. **Grill the Steak:**
    - Preheat a grill or a grill pan over medium-high heat.
    - Remove the steak from the marinade and grill for about 4-6 minutes per side, depending on the thickness and desired level of doneness.
    - Once cooked, let the steak rest for a few minutes before slicing it thinly against the grain.

## 2. Prepare the Huaraches:

1. **Mix the Dough:**
   - In a large bowl, combine masa harina, salt, and warm water. Mix until a soft dough forms. You might need to adjust the water amount to get the right consistency. If the dough is too dry, add more water a little at a time. If too sticky, add a bit more masa harina.
2. **Shape the Huaraches:**
   - Divide the dough into 6-8 equal portions.
   - Using a rolling pin or a tortilla press, shape each portion into an oval or teardrop shape, about 1/4 inch thick. You can also shape them by hand if you don't have a press.
3. **Cook the Huaraches:**
   - Heat a griddle or large skillet over medium-high heat.
   - Cook each huarache for about 1-2 minutes on each side, until they are lightly browned and cooked through. The surface should have small brown spots.

## 3. Assemble the Huaraches:

1. **Top with Carne Asada:**
   - Place the cooked huaraches on a serving plate.
   - Top each huarache with slices of grilled carne asada.
2. **Add Toppings:**
   - Add shredded lettuce or cabbage, diced tomatoes, sliced onions, chopped cilantro, crumbled queso fresco, and a dollop of sour cream or Mexican crema.
   - Finish with your favorite salsa or hot sauce.

Serve the huaraches de carne asada warm, and enjoy this flavorful and satisfying Mexican dish!

**Enchiladas de Mole**

## Ingredients

**For the Mole Sauce:**

- 4 dried ancho chilies
- 4 dried pasilla chilies
- 1 tablespoon vegetable oil
- 1 medium onion, chopped
- 3 cloves garlic, minced
- 1/2 cup almonds (or peanuts)
- 1/4 cup sesame seeds
- 1/4 cup raisins
- 2 tablespoons cocoa powder
- 1 teaspoon ground cumin
- 1 teaspoon dried oregano
- 1/2 teaspoon ground cinnamon
- 1/4 teaspoon ground cloves
- 2 cups chicken or vegetable broth
- 1 tablespoon tomato paste
- Salt to taste
- 1 tablespoon sugar (optional, to taste)

**For the Enchiladas:**

- 12 corn tortillas
- 2 cups cooked, shredded chicken or beef (optional)
- 1 cup shredded cheese (optional, for topping)
- 1/2 cup finely chopped onion (for garnish)
- 1/4 cup chopped fresh cilantro (for garnish)

## Instructions

**1. Prepare the Mole Sauce:**

1. **Toast the Chilies:**
    - Remove the stems and seeds from the dried chilies.
    - Heat a skillet over medium heat and toast the chilies for about 30 seconds on each side until fragrant. Be careful not to burn them.
2. **Soak the Chilies:**
    - Place the toasted chilies in a bowl and cover them with hot water. Let them soak for about 20 minutes until they are softened.
3. **Blend the Sauce:**
    - Drain the chilies and place them in a blender. Add a bit of the soaking water to help with blending.
    - Blend until smooth, adding more water if necessary. Set the chili paste aside.
4. **Cook the Mole Sauce:**
    - In a large saucepan, heat the vegetable oil over medium heat.
    - Add the chopped onion and cook until translucent, about 5 minutes.
    - Add the minced garlic and cook for another minute.

- Add the almonds, sesame seeds, raisins, and cook for 2-3 minutes, stirring frequently.
- Stir in the chili paste, cocoa powder, cumin, oregano, cinnamon, and cloves. Cook for 5 minutes, stirring often.
- Add the broth and tomato paste, and bring to a simmer. Reduce the heat and let it simmer gently for about 30 minutes, stirring occasionally. The sauce should be thickened and flavorful.
- Season with salt to taste and adjust the sweetness with sugar if needed.

### 2. Prepare the Enchiladas:

1. **Prepare the Tortillas:**
   - Warm the corn tortillas in a dry skillet or on a comal until pliable. You can also wrap them in a damp cloth and microwave them for about 30 seconds.
2. **Fill the Enchiladas:**
   - Dip each tortilla in the mole sauce to coat it lightly.
   - Place a portion of shredded chicken or beef in the center of each tortilla.
   - Roll up the tortilla and place it seam-side down in a baking dish.
3. **Assemble the Dish:**
   - Once all the tortillas are filled and placed in the baking dish, pour additional mole sauce over the top, making sure each enchilada is well coated.
   - Sprinkle shredded cheese on top if using.
4. **Bake (optional):**
   - If you want to melt the cheese and heat everything through, bake in a preheated oven at 350°F (175°C) for about 15-20 minutes.
5. **Garnish and Serve:**
   - Garnish with finely chopped onion and fresh cilantro.
   - Serve with rice and beans or a side salad for a complete meal.

Enjoy your homemade enchiladas de mole, rich in flavor and perfect for a comforting meal!

Salsa Verde Cruda

## Ingredients:

- **8-10 medium tomatillos** (husks removed and rinsed)
- **2-3 serrano or jalapeño peppers** (adjust for heat preference)
- **1 small onion**, finely chopped
- **1/2 cup fresh cilantro**, chopped
- **2 cloves garlic**, minced
- **1 lime**, juiced
- **Salt to taste**
- **Optional: 1 avocado**, diced (for added creaminess)

## Instructions:

1. **Prepare the Tomatillos and Peppers:**
   - Cut the tomatillos into quarters.
   - If you prefer a milder salsa, remove the seeds from the peppers; otherwise, leave them in for more heat.
2. **Blend the Ingredients:**
   - In a blender or food processor, combine the quartered tomatillos, peppers, and minced garlic.
   - Blend until smooth or until you reach your desired consistency. Some prefer a chunkier salsa, so blend less if that's the case.
3. **Mix in Fresh Ingredients:**
   - Transfer the blended mixture to a bowl.
   - Stir in the finely chopped onion, chopped cilantro, and lime juice.
   - Season with salt to taste.
4. **Optional Avocado Addition:**
   - If using, gently fold in the diced avocado for extra creaminess.
5. **Chill and Serve:**
   - Let the salsa sit for about 30 minutes to allow the flavors to meld.
   - Serve with tortilla chips, tacos, grilled meats, or as a topping for various dishes.

## Tips:

- **Adjust Heat:** Serrano peppers are spicier than jalapeños, so adjust according to your taste. You can also use a combination of both.
- **Tomatillo Prep:** Tomatillos should be firm and bright green. If they're overly soft or discolored, they might be past their prime.
- **Storage:** Salsa verde cruda can be stored in an airtight container in the refrigerator for up to a week.

Enjoy your fresh and tangy salsa verde cruda!

**Tacos de Pescado**

## Ingredients:

**For the Fish:**

- 1 lb (450 g) white fish fillets (such as cod, tilapia, or halibut)

- 1 cup all-purpose flour
- 1/2 cup cornmeal (optional, for extra crunch)
- 1 teaspoon paprika
- 1 teaspoon garlic powder
- 1 teaspoon onion powder
- 1/2 teaspoon cayenne pepper (optional, for heat)
- 1 teaspoon salt
- 1/2 teaspoon black pepper
- 1 egg
- 1 cup buttermilk (or milk with a tablespoon of lemon juice)
- Vegetable oil (for frying)

**For the Tacos:**

- 8-10 small corn or flour tortillas
- Shredded cabbage or lettuce
- Sliced radishes
- Diced tomatoes
- Chopped cilantro
- Lime wedges (for serving)

**For the Sauce (optional):**

- 1/2 cup sour cream or Mexican crema
- 2 tablespoons mayonnaise
- 1 tablespoon lime juice
- 1 tablespoon chopped fresh cilantro
- 1 teaspoon hot sauce (adjust to taste)
- Salt to taste

## Instructions:

### 1. Prepare the Fish:

1. **Cut and Season:**
   - Cut the fish fillets into bite-sized strips or pieces.
   - Season the fish with a little salt and pepper.
2. **Prepare the Breading:**
   - In a shallow dish, mix the flour, cornmeal, paprika, garlic powder, onion powder, cayenne pepper, salt, and black pepper.
   - In another bowl, whisk together the egg and buttermilk.
3. **Bread the Fish:**
   - Dip each piece of fish into the buttermilk mixture, then coat it with the flour mixture, pressing lightly to adhere.
4. **Fry the Fish:**

- Heat about 1 inch of vegetable oil in a large skillet over medium-high heat. The oil should be hot but not smoking.
- Fry the fish pieces in batches, being careful not to overcrowd the pan, for about 2-3 minutes per side, or until golden brown and cooked through. Use a slotted spoon to transfer the fish to a paper towel-lined plate to drain excess oil.

**2. Prepare the Sauce (optional):**

1. **Mix Ingredients:**
   - In a small bowl, combine sour cream (or Mexican crema), mayonnaise, lime juice, chopped cilantro, hot sauce, and salt. Mix until smooth.

**3. Assemble the Tacos:**

1. **Warm the Tortillas:**
   - Warm the tortillas in a dry skillet, on a comal, or in the oven until pliable.
2. **Assemble:**
   - Place a few pieces of crispy fish onto each tortilla.
   - Top with shredded cabbage or lettuce, sliced radishes, diced tomatoes, and chopped cilantro.
3. **Add Sauce:**
   - Drizzle with the prepared sauce if using, or serve it on the side.
4. **Serve:**
   - Garnish with lime wedges for a fresh squeeze of lime juice.

Enjoy your homemade tacos de pescado! They're perfect for a light and flavorful meal, and you can adjust the toppings and sauce to your taste.

**Pibil Tacos**

**Ingredients:**

**For the Marinade:**

- 1/4 cup apple cider vinegar

- 1/4 cup orange juice
- 1/4 cup pineapple juice
- 3 cloves garlic, minced
- 2 tablespoons adobo sauce (from a can of chipotles in adobo)
- 1 tablespoon ground chili powder
- 1 tablespoon paprika
- 1 teaspoon ground cumin
- 1 teaspoon dried oregano
- 1/2 teaspoon ground cinnamon
- 1/4 teaspoon ground cloves
- 1/2 teaspoon salt
- 1/4 teaspoon black pepper

**For the Pork:**

- 2 lbs (900 g) pork shoulder or pork butt, thinly sliced
- 2 tablespoons vegetable oil (for grilling or cooking)
- Pineapple slices, for grilling

**For the Tacos:**

- Corn tortillas
- Finely chopped onions
- Chopped fresh cilantro
- Lime wedges
- Salsa (optional, for serving)

## Instructions:

### 1. Prepare the Marinade:

1. **Mix Ingredients:**
   - In a bowl, combine the apple cider vinegar, orange juice, pineapple juice, minced garlic, adobo sauce, chili powder, paprika, cumin, oregano, cinnamon, cloves, salt, and pepper. Stir until well combined.
2. **Marinate the Pork:**
   - Place the sliced pork in a large resealable plastic bag or a bowl.
   - Pour the marinade over the pork and mix well to ensure all pieces are coated.
   - Seal the bag or cover the bowl and refrigerate for at least 4 hours, preferably overnight for maximum flavor.

### 2. Cook the Pork:

1. **Grill or Pan-Fry:**
   - Preheat your grill or a large skillet over medium-high heat. If using a grill, oil the grates to prevent sticking.

- Remove the pork from the marinade, allowing excess to drip off.
- Cook the pork slices on the grill or in the skillet for about 3-4 minutes per side, or until well browned and cooked through. If grilling, you can also add pineapple slices to the grill and cook until caramelized.

2. **Slice the Pork:**
    - After cooking, let the pork rest for a few minutes before slicing it thinly or chopping it into bite-sized pieces.

### 3. Assemble the Tacos:

1. **Warm the Tortillas:**
    - Heat the corn tortillas on a comal or in a dry skillet until they are warm and pliable.
2. **Build the Tacos:**
    - Place some of the cooked pork on each tortilla.
    - Top with finely chopped onions, fresh cilantro, and a squeeze of lime juice.
3. **Add Optional Salsa:**
    - Add salsa if desired for extra flavor.

### 4. Serve:

- Serve the tacos immediately while they're warm, with extra lime wedges and salsa on the side.

Enjoy your tacos al pastor, bursting with the vibrant and tangy flavors of Mexico! If you meant cochinita pibil or another type of taco, just let me know.

**Mexican Street Corn (Elote)**

## Ingredients:

- 4 ears of corn, husked and cleaned
- 1/2 cup mayonnaise
- 1/4 cup sour cream

- 1/2 cup crumbled queso fresco (or cotija cheese)
- 2 tablespoons lime juice (about 1 lime)
- 1 teaspoon chili powder (or to taste)
- 1/2 teaspoon smoked paprika (optional, for extra flavor)
- 1/2 teaspoon garlic powder
- 1/2 teaspoon onion powder
- Salt to taste
- Fresh cilantro, chopped (for garnish)
- Extra lime wedges, for serving

## Instructions:

**1. Grill the Corn:**

1. **Preheat Grill:**
   - Preheat your grill to medium-high heat.
2. **Grill Corn:**
   - Place the cleaned corn directly on the grill grates.
   - Grill the corn for about 10-15 minutes, turning occasionally, until all sides are evenly charred and the kernels are tender. The exact grilling time will depend on the heat of your grill and the size of the corn.

**2. Prepare the Sauce:**

1. **Mix Ingredients:**
   - In a bowl, combine the mayonnaise, sour cream, and lime juice. Mix until smooth.
   - Stir in the garlic powder, onion powder, and smoked paprika (if using). Adjust the seasoning with salt to taste.

**3. Assemble the Elote:**

1. **Coat the Corn:**
   - Once the corn is grilled, remove it from the grill and let it cool slightly.
   - Using a brush or spoon, generously coat each ear of corn with the prepared sauce.
2. **Add Toppings:**
   - Sprinkle the crumbled queso fresco (or cotija cheese) over the sauced corn.
   - Dust with chili powder to taste. You can adjust the amount depending on your heat preference.
3. **Garnish:**
   - Garnish with chopped fresh cilantro.
4. **Serve:**
   - Serve the elote with extra lime wedges on the side for an additional squeeze of lime juice.

## Tips:

- **Cheese Options:** If you can't find queso fresco or cotija cheese, you can use Parmesan cheese as a substitute, though it will be a bit different in flavor.
- **Adjusting Spice:** Feel free to adjust the amount of chili powder based on your preference for spiciness.
- **Corn Freshness:** Fresh corn is best for this recipe, but you can use frozen corn if fresh is not available. Just be sure to thaw and pat it dry before grilling.

Enjoy this delicious, savory, and tangy Mexican street corn as a fantastic side dish or a tasty snack!

**Tamale Pie**

## Ingredients

**For the Meat Mixture:**

- 1 lb (450 g) ground beef (or ground pork or turkey)

- 1 onion, finely chopped
- 2 cloves garlic, minced
- 1 red bell pepper, diced
- 1 can (14.5 oz) diced tomatoes (with green chilies, if you like some heat)
- 1 can (8 oz) tomato sauce
- 1/2 cup frozen or canned corn kernels
- 1/2 cup black beans (drained and rinsed, optional)
- 1 tablespoon chili powder
- 1 teaspoon ground cumin
- 1 teaspoon paprika
- 1/2 teaspoon dried oregano
- Salt and pepper to taste

**For the Cornbread Topping:**

- 1 cup cornmeal
- 1 cup all-purpose flour
- 1/4 cup sugar
- 1 tablespoon baking powder
- 1/2 teaspoon salt
- 1 cup milk
- 1/4 cup vegetable oil
- 1 large egg
- 1 cup shredded cheddar cheese (optional, for extra flavor)

## Instructions

### 1. Prepare the Meat Mixture:

1. **Cook the Meat:**
   - In a large skillet or oven-safe pan, cook the ground beef over medium heat until it starts to brown, breaking it up with a spoon as it cooks.
2. **Add Vegetables:**
   - Add the chopped onion, garlic, and red bell pepper to the skillet. Cook until the vegetables are softened, about 5 minutes.
3. **Add Sauces and Seasonings:**
   - Stir in the diced tomatoes, tomato sauce, corn kernels, and black beans (if using).
   - Add the chili powder, cumin, paprika, oregano, salt, and pepper. Mix well and let simmer for about 10 minutes, allowing the flavors to meld together.

### 2. Prepare the Cornbread Topping:

1. **Mix Dry Ingredients:**
   - In a large bowl, combine the cornmeal, flour, sugar, baking powder, and salt.

2. **Mix Wet Ingredients:**
   - In another bowl, whisk together the milk, vegetable oil, and egg.
3. **Combine:**
   - Pour the wet ingredients into the dry ingredients and stir until just combined. Fold in the shredded cheddar cheese if using.

### 3. Assemble and Bake:

1. **Preheat Oven:**
   - Preheat your oven to 400°F (200°C).
2. **Assemble the Pie:**
   - Spread the meat mixture evenly in the bottom of an oven-safe baking dish (such as a 9-inch pie dish or an 8x8-inch square baking dish).
   - Pour the cornbread batter evenly over the top of the meat mixture, spreading it out with a spatula to cover the filling completely.
3. **Bake:**
   - Bake in the preheated oven for about 25-30 minutes, or until the cornbread topping is golden brown and a toothpick inserted into the center comes out clean.
4. **Cool and Serve:**
   - Let the tamale pie cool for a few minutes before serving. This allows the filling to set and makes it easier to cut into portions.

## Tips:

- **Vegetarian Option:** You can substitute the ground meat with a mix of vegetables like mushrooms, zucchini, and bell peppers for a vegetarian version.
- **Add Spice:** For extra heat, consider adding some diced jalapeños to the meat mixture or sprinkling some hot sauce on top before baking.
- **Serving Suggestions:** Serve with a side of sour cream, salsa, or a simple green salad for a complete meal.

Enjoy your tamale pie as a hearty and satisfying meal that brings the flavors of tamales into an easy-to-make casserole!

**Mexican Beef Stew**

## Ingredients:

- 2 lbs (900 g) beef chuck or stew meat, cut into bite-sized cubes
- 2 tablespoons vegetable oil
- 1 large onion, chopped
- 3 cloves garlic, minced
- 1 bell pepper (red or green), chopped
- 2 large tomatoes, chopped (or 1 can (14.5 oz) diced tomatoes)
- 1 cup beef broth (or water)
- 1/2 cup tomato sauce
- 1 tablespoon chili powder
- 1 teaspoon ground cumin
- 1 teaspoon paprika
- 1/2 teaspoon dried oregano
- 1/2 teaspoon ground black pepper
- 1 teaspoon salt (adjust to taste)
- 2 medium potatoes, peeled and diced
- 2 medium carrots, peeled and sliced
- 1/2 cup frozen peas (optional)
- 1 bay leaf
- 1/4 cup chopped fresh cilantro (for garnish)
- Lime wedges (for serving)

## Instructions:

### 1. Brown the Beef:

1. **Heat Oil:**
   - In a large pot or Dutch oven, heat the vegetable oil over medium-high heat.
2. **Brown Beef:**
   - Add the beef cubes in batches, making sure not to overcrowd the pot. Brown the beef on all sides, then transfer to a plate. Repeat until all the beef is browned.

### 2. Cook Vegetables:

1. **Sauté Onions and Garlic:**
   - In the same pot, add the chopped onions and cook until they are soft and translucent, about 5 minutes.
   - Add the minced garlic and cook for another minute, until fragrant.
2. **Add Bell Pepper and Tomatoes:**
   - Stir in the chopped bell pepper and tomatoes (or diced tomatoes). Cook for another 5 minutes, allowing the vegetables to soften and the tomatoes to break down.

### 3. Add Spices and Broth:

1. **Mix in Spices:**
   - Stir in the chili powder, cumin, paprika, oregano, black pepper, and salt.
2. **Add Beef and Liquids:**
   - Return the browned beef to the pot. Add the beef broth, tomato sauce, and bay leaf. Stir to combine.
3. **Simmer:**
   - Bring the mixture to a boil, then reduce the heat to low. Cover and let simmer for about 1 to 1.5 hours, or until the beef is tender and the flavors are well combined.

### 4. Add Vegetables:

1. **Add Potatoes and Carrots:**
   - Stir in the diced potatoes and sliced carrots. Continue to simmer, uncovered, for about 30 minutes, or until the potatoes and carrots are tender.
2. **Add Peas (Optional):**
   - If using frozen peas, stir them in during the last 5 minutes of cooking.

### 5. Final Touches:

1. **Adjust Seasoning:**
   - Taste and adjust seasoning with more salt and pepper if needed.
2. **Garnish and Serve:**
   - Remove the bay leaf. Garnish the stew with chopped fresh cilantro.
   - Serve hot with lime wedges on the side for an extra burst of flavor.

## Tips:

- **Thickening:** If you prefer a thicker stew, you can mash some of the potatoes against the side of the pot or stir in a slurry of cornstarch and water (1 tablespoon cornstarch mixed with 2 tablespoons water) during the last 10 minutes of cooking.
- **Spicy Option:** For added heat, you can include diced jalapeños or a pinch of cayenne pepper.
- **Slow Cooker Option:** You can also prepare this stew in a slow cooker. Brown the beef and sauté the onions and garlic first, then transfer everything to the slow cooker. Cook on low for 6-8 hours or high for 3-4 hours.

Enjoy your hearty and flavorful Mexican beef stew, perfect for a cozy meal!

**Churros con Chocolate**

## Ingredients

**For the Churros:**

- 1 cup water
- 1/2 cup unsalted butter
- 1/4 teaspoon salt
- 1 cup all-purpose flour
- 2 large eggs
- 1 teaspoon vanilla extract
- 1/2 cup granulated sugar (for coating)
- 1 tablespoon ground cinnamon (for coating)

**For the Chocolate Sauce:**

- 1 cup heavy cream
- 4 oz (115 g) semisweet or bittersweet chocolate, chopped (or chocolate chips)
- 1 tablespoon granulated sugar (optional, to taste)
- 1/2 teaspoon vanilla extract

## Instructions

### 1. Prepare the Churros:

1. **Preheat Oil:**
   - In a large, heavy-bottomed pot or deep fryer, heat about 2 inches of vegetable oil to 350°F (175°C). Use a candy thermometer to monitor the temperature.
2. **Make the Dough:**
   - In a medium saucepan, combine the water, butter, and salt. Bring to a boil over medium heat.
   - Once the butter has melted and the mixture is boiling, remove from heat and stir in the flour all at once. Mix vigorously until the dough comes together and starts to pull away from the sides of the pan.
   - Allow the dough to cool for a few minutes, then beat in the eggs one at a time until fully incorporated. Stir in the vanilla extract. The dough should be smooth and slightly sticky.
3. **Pipe the Churros:**
   - Transfer the dough to a piping bag fitted with a star tip (or a large zip-top bag with the corner cut off).
   - Pipe strips of dough into the hot oil, cutting them to your desired length with scissors or a knife. Fry in batches, being careful not to overcrowd the pot.

- Fry the churros for 2-3 minutes on each side, or until golden brown and crispy.
4. **Drain and Coat:**
   - Remove the churros from the oil with a slotted spoon and drain on paper towels.
   - While still warm, roll the churros in a mixture of granulated sugar and ground cinnamon.

## 2. Prepare the Chocolate Sauce:

1. **Heat Cream:**
   - In a small saucepan, heat the heavy cream over medium heat until it just begins to simmer.
2. **Add Chocolate:**
   - Remove from heat and add the chopped chocolate. Let it sit for a minute, then stir until smooth and fully melted. If using chocolate chips, stir until melted and smooth.
3. **Sweeten and Flavor:**
   - Stir in the granulated sugar if desired, and add the vanilla extract. Mix well.

## 3. Serve:

- Serve the churros warm with the chocolate sauce for dipping.

# Tips:

- **Consistency of Dough:** If the dough seems too thick or dry, you can add a bit of milk. If it's too thin, add a little more flour.
- **Frying:** Ensure the oil temperature stays consistent. If the oil is too hot, the churros will brown too quickly on the outside and remain raw inside. If it's too cool, they'll absorb too much oil and become greasy.
- **Serving:** Churros are best enjoyed fresh. You can keep them warm in a low oven if necessary, but they may lose some crispiness.

Enjoy your homemade churros con chocolate, a delightful treat that's perfect for sharing or enjoying on your own!

**Tres Leches Cake**

## Ingredients

### For the Cake:

- 1 cup all-purpose flour
- 1 1/2 teaspoons baking powder
- 1/4 teaspoon salt
- 1/2 cup unsalted butter (room temperature)
- 1 cup granulated sugar
- 5 large eggs
- 1 teaspoon vanilla extract
- 1/2 cup whole milk

### For the Milk Soak:

- 1 can (14 oz) sweetened condensed milk
- 1 can (12 oz) evaporated milk
- 1/2 cup whole milk
- 1 teaspoon vanilla extract

### For the Topping:

- 1 cup heavy cream
- 2 tablespoons granulated sugar
- 1 teaspoon vanilla extract
- Fresh fruit (such as strawberries, raspberries, or peaches, optional)

## Instructions

### 1. Prepare the Cake:

1. **Preheat Oven:**
   - Preheat your oven to 350°F (175°C). Grease and flour a 9x13-inch baking dish or a similar-sized pan.
2. **Mix Dry Ingredients:**
   - In a medium bowl, whisk together the flour, baking powder, and salt. Set aside.
3. **Cream Butter and Sugar:**
   - In a large bowl, beat the butter and sugar together with an electric mixer until light and fluffy, about 3-4 minutes.
4. **Add Eggs and Vanilla:**

- Beat in the eggs one at a time, making sure each egg is fully incorporated before adding the next.
- Mix in the vanilla extract.
5. **Combine Ingredients:**
    - Gradually add the dry ingredients to the butter mixture, alternating with the milk. Begin and end with the flour mixture. Mix just until combined; be careful not to overmix.
6. **Bake:**
    - Pour the batter into the prepared baking dish and spread it evenly.
    - Bake for 25-30 minutes, or until a toothpick inserted into the center comes out clean.
7. **Cool:**
    - Allow the cake to cool in the pan on a wire rack for about 10 minutes.

## 2. Prepare the Milk Soak:

1. **Mix Soak Ingredients:**
    - In a bowl or measuring cup, combine the sweetened condensed milk, evaporated milk, whole milk, and vanilla extract. Stir well.
2. **Soak the Cake:**
    - Once the cake has cooled for 10 minutes, use a fork or skewer to poke holes all over the surface of the cake.
    - Slowly pour the milk mixture over the cake, making sure it soaks in evenly. You may need to let the cake sit for about 30 minutes to fully absorb the milk mixture.

## 3. Prepare the Topping:

1. **Whip Cream:**
    - In a medium bowl, beat the heavy cream, sugar, and vanilla extract with an electric mixer until stiff peaks form.
2. **Frost Cake:**
    - Spread the whipped cream over the top of the cake, smoothing it out with a spatula.
3. **Add Fruit (Optional):**
    - Garnish with fresh fruit if desired.

## 4. Serve:

- Refrigerate the cake for at least 2 hours before serving, or overnight. The cake will continue to absorb the milk mixture as it sits, becoming even more moist and flavorful.

Enjoy your Tres Leches Cake, a wonderfully indulgent dessert that's perfect for special occasions or as a sweet treat any time!

# Coconut Flan

## Ingredients

### For the Caramel:

- 1 cup granulated sugar
- 1/4 cup water

### For the Flan:

- 1 can (14 oz) sweetened condensed milk
- 1 can (12 oz) evaporated milk
- 1 cup full-fat coconut milk
- 4 large eggs
- 1 tablespoon vanilla extract
- 1/2 cup shredded sweetened coconut (optional, for extra coconut flavor and texture)

## Instructions

### 1. Prepare the Caramel:

1. **Heat Sugar:**
   - In a medium saucepan over medium heat, combine the granulated sugar and water. Stir gently until the sugar has dissolved.
2. **Cook Caramel:**
   - Increase the heat to medium-high and bring the mixture to a boil. Do not stir, but gently swirl the pan occasionally. Cook until the syrup turns a deep amber color (about 8-10 minutes). Be careful not to burn it.
3. **Pour Caramel:**
   - Quickly and carefully pour the hot caramel into the bottom of a 9-inch round baking dish or a flan mold, tilting the dish to coat the bottom evenly. Set aside to cool and harden.

### 2. Prepare the Flan Mixture:

1. **Mix Ingredients:**
   - In a large bowl, whisk together the sweetened condensed milk, evaporated milk, coconut milk, eggs, and vanilla extract until smooth and well combined.
2. **Add Shredded Coconut:**
   - If using, stir in the shredded coconut.

### 3. Bake the Flan:

1. **Preheat Oven:**
   - Preheat your oven to 325°F (160°C).
2. **Prepare Water Bath:**
   - Place the caramel-coated baking dish or flan mold inside a larger baking pan. Pour hot water into the larger pan until it reaches halfway up the sides of the flan dish. This creates a water bath to gently cook the flan.
3. **Pour and Bake:**
   - Carefully pour the flan mixture over the hardened caramel in the baking dish.
   - Bake in the preheated oven for 50-60 minutes, or until the flan is set and a knife inserted into the center comes out clean. The center should be slightly jiggly but firm.

**4. Cool and Serve:**

1. **Cool Flan:**
   - Remove the flan from the water bath and let it cool to room temperature.
   - Cover and refrigerate for at least 4 hours, preferably overnight, to fully set and allow the flavors to meld.
2. **Unmold and Serve:**
   - To unmold the flan, run a knife around the edges to loosen it. Place a large plate over the baking dish and invert to release the flan. The caramel sauce will flow over the top of the flan.
3. **Garnish (Optional):**
   - Garnish with additional shredded coconut or fresh fruit if desired.

## Tips:

- **Caramelizing Sugar:** Watch the sugar closely as it caramelizes. It can go from golden to burnt very quickly.
- **Straining Mixture:** For an extra smooth texture, strain the flan mixture through a fine-mesh sieve before pouring it into the baking dish.
- **Storage:** Store leftover flan covered in the refrigerator for up to 5 days.

Enjoy your homemade coconut flan, a tropical twist on a classic dessert that's sure to impress!

**Mexican Hot Chocolate**

## Ingredients

- **2 cups whole milk** (or any milk of your choice)
- **1/2 cup water**
- **1 tablet Mexican chocolate** (such as Abuelita or Ibarra) or 1/2 cup chopped Mexican chocolate
- **2 tablespoons granulated sugar** (optional, adjust to taste)
- **1/2 teaspoon ground cinnamon** (optional, for extra spice)
- **1/4 teaspoon vanilla extract** (optional)
- **Whipped cream or marshmallows** (for topping, optional)

## Instructions

### 1. Heat the Milk and Water:

1. **Combine Liquids:**
   - In a medium saucepan, combine the whole milk and water. Heat over medium heat until it starts to warm up but is not boiling.

### 2. Add Chocolate:

1. **Stir in Chocolate:**
   - Break the Mexican chocolate tablet into pieces and add it to the warm milk mixture. If using chopped Mexican chocolate, add it to the saucepan.
2. **Dissolve Chocolate:**
   - Stir continuously until the chocolate is completely melted and fully incorporated into the milk. This can take a few minutes. The mixture should be smooth and creamy.

### 3. Flavor the Hot Chocolate:

1. **Add Sugar and Cinnamon:**
   - Taste the hot chocolate. If you prefer it sweeter, stir in granulated sugar to taste. You can also add ground cinnamon for an extra layer of spice.
2. **Add Vanilla Extract:**
   - Stir in vanilla extract if desired.

### 4. Froth the Hot Chocolate (Optional):

1. **Froth for Texture:**
   - For a traditional Mexican touch, you can froth the hot chocolate using a molinillo (a traditional Mexican whisk) or a milk frother. If using a molinillo, place it

between your hands and spin it back and forth while holding it in the hot chocolate to create a frothy top.

### 5. Serve:

1. **Pour and Enjoy:**
   - Pour the hot chocolate into mugs. Top with whipped cream or marshmallows if desired.

## Tips:

- **Mexican Chocolate Tablets:** If you can't find Mexican chocolate tablets, you can use high-quality semisweet or bittersweet chocolate and add a bit of ground cinnamon and a pinch of chili powder for a similar flavor profile.
- **Spicy Variation:** For a spicier version, add a pinch of cayenne pepper or chili powder.
- **Creamier Hot Chocolate:** For an even creamier drink, you can use half-and-half or add a splash of heavy cream.

Enjoy your Mexican hot chocolate, a perfect treat for cozying up on a chilly day or as a sweet indulgence any time!

**Chicken Pozole**

## Ingredients

**For the Pozole:**

- **1.5 lbs (680 g) chicken thighs** or chicken breasts (bone-in, skinless preferred)
- **1 tablespoon vegetable oil**
- **1 large onion**, chopped
- **3 cloves garlic**, minced
- **1 can (15 oz) hominy**, drained and rinsed (or 2 cups dried hominy, soaked and cooked)
- **4 cups chicken broth** (or water)
- **1 can (14.5 oz) diced tomatoes** (with or without green chilies, depending on your heat preference)
- **1-2 dried ancho chiles**, seeds and stems removed (or 1-2 tablespoons of ancho chili powder)
- **1-2 dried guajillo chiles**, seeds and stems removed (or 1-2 tablespoons of guajillo chili powder)
- **1 teaspoon ground cumin**
- **1 teaspoon dried oregano**
- **1 bay leaf**
- **Salt and black pepper** to taste
- **1-2 tablespoons lime juice** (to taste)

**For Garnishing:**

- **Shredded cabbage** or lettuce
- **Sliced radishes**
- **Chopped fresh cilantro**
- **Diced avocado**
- **Lime wedges**
- **Diced onions**
- **Sliced jalapeños** (optional, for extra heat)
- **Tostadas or tortilla chips** (for serving)

## Instructions

### 1. Prepare the Chicken:

1. **Cook Chicken:**
    - In a large pot or Dutch oven, heat the vegetable oil over medium heat.
    - Add the chicken thighs or breasts and cook until browned on both sides (about 5-7 minutes per side). Remove the chicken from the pot and set aside.

## 2. Make the Base:

1. **Sauté Aromatics:**
   - In the same pot, add the chopped onion and cook until softened, about 5 minutes.
   - Add the minced garlic and cook for another minute until fragrant.
2. **Prepare Chiles (if using dried chiles):**
   - If using dried chiles, toast them in a dry skillet over medium heat for about 1-2 minutes until they become aromatic. Be careful not to burn them.
   - After toasting, place the chiles in a bowl and cover with hot water. Let them soak for about 15 minutes until softened. Drain and blend into a smooth paste with a bit of water, or use a blender or food processor.
3. **Add Ingredients:**
   - Stir in the diced tomatoes, chiles (or chili powder), ground cumin, dried oregano, and bay leaf.
   - Cook for a few minutes, allowing the flavors to meld together.

## 3. Simmer the Pozole:

1. **Add Broth and Hominy:**
   - Return the browned chicken to the pot. Add the chicken broth and hominy.
   - Bring to a boil, then reduce the heat to low. Cover and simmer for about 30-40 minutes, or until the chicken is cooked through and tender.
2. **Shred the Chicken:**
   - Remove the chicken from the pot and shred it into bite-sized pieces using two forks. Return the shredded chicken to the pot.
3. **Season:**
   - Taste the pozole and adjust seasoning with salt, black pepper, and lime juice. If the pozole is too thick, you can add more chicken broth or water to reach your desired consistency.

## 4. Serve:

1. **Prepare Garnishes:**
   - Arrange the shredded cabbage, sliced radishes, chopped cilantro, diced avocado, lime wedges, and diced onions on a platter for guests to garnish their own bowls.
2. **Serve:**
   - Ladle the hot pozole into bowls and serve with the assorted garnishes and tortilla chips or tostadas on the side.

# Tips:

- **Hominy:** If using dried hominy, make sure it's fully cooked before adding it to the pozole. This can take several hours, so plan ahead or use canned hominy for a quicker option.

- **Adjust Spice Levels:** Adjust the amount of chili powder or dried chiles according to your heat preference.
- **Garnishes:** The fresh garnishes add a lot of flavor and texture to the pozole, so don't skip them!

Enjoy your Chicken Pozole, a warm and hearty dish that's perfect for family gatherings or a comforting meal any day of the week!

**Queso Fundido con Chorizo**

## Ingredients

- **1/2 lb (225 g) Mexican chorizo** (or Spanish chorizo if Mexican chorizo is unavailable), casing removed
- **2 cups shredded cheese** (such as Oaxaca, Chihuahua, or a mix of Monterey Jack and cheddar)
- **1 tablespoon vegetable oil**
- **1 small onion**, finely chopped
- **2 cloves garlic**, minced
- **1 small tomato**, diced
- **1/4 cup chopped fresh cilantro** (optional, for garnish)
- **1/2 teaspoon ground cumin** (optional)
- **1/4 teaspoon red pepper flakes** (optional, for extra heat)
- **Tortillas, tortilla chips, or crusty bread** (for serving)

## Instructions

### 1. Cook the Chorizo:

1. **Heat Oil:**
   - In a large skillet, heat the vegetable oil over medium heat.
2. **Cook Chorizo:**
   - Add the chorizo to the skillet, breaking it up with a spoon as it cooks. Cook until the chorizo is fully browned and cooked through, about 5-7 minutes.
3. **Remove Excess Fat:**
   - Once the chorizo is cooked, use a slotted spoon to transfer it to a plate, leaving any excess fat in the skillet. Set the chorizo aside.

### 2. Prepare the Cheese Mixture:

1. **Sauté Vegetables:**
   - In the same skillet with the remaining fat, add the chopped onion and cook until softened, about 3-4 minutes.
   - Add the minced garlic and cook for another minute until fragrant.
   - Stir in the diced tomato and cook for an additional 2 minutes.
2. **Add Cheese:**
   - Reduce the heat to low. Return the cooked chorizo to the skillet, mixing it with the sautéed vegetables.
   - Add the shredded cheese on top. Stir occasionally until the cheese is melted and bubbly, about 5-7 minutes. If needed, you can cover the skillet with a lid to help the cheese melt more evenly.

**3. Garnish and Serve:**

1. **Garnish:**
   - If desired, stir in chopped fresh cilantro and season with ground cumin and red pepper flakes for extra flavor.
2. **Serve:**
   - Serve the queso fundido hot, straight from the skillet. Accompany with tortillas, tortilla chips, or crusty bread for dipping.

## Tips:

- **Cheese Variety:** For the best melt and flavor, use a combination of cheeses that melt well, such as Oaxaca, Chihuahua, Monterey Jack, or cheddar. You can also use a pre-shredded cheese blend for convenience.
- **Serving:** Queso fundido is best enjoyed immediately while it's still warm and gooey. It can be served as an appetizer, party dip, or a topping for tacos or burritos.
- **Additions:** You can add other ingredients such as sautéed peppers, mushrooms, or even some jalapeños for added flavor and texture.

Enjoy your Queso Fundido con Chorizo, a creamy, cheesy, and spicy delight that's sure to be a hit with family and friends!

**Mexican Rice**

## Ingredients

- 1 cup long-grain white rice
- 2 tablespoons vegetable oil (or any cooking oil)
- 1 small onion, finely chopped
- 2 cloves garlic, minced
- 1 can (14.5 oz) diced tomatoes (or 1 1/2 cups fresh tomatoes, finely chopped)
- 1 cup chicken broth (or vegetable broth for a vegetarian option)
- 1/2 cup water
- 1 teaspoon ground cumin
- 1/2 teaspoon chili powder (optional, for extra flavor)
- 1/2 teaspoon paprika (optional, for color and flavor)
- 1 bay leaf
- Salt and black pepper to taste
- 1/2 cup frozen peas (optional, for added color and nutrition)
- 1/4 cup chopped fresh cilantro (optional, for garnish)

## Instructions

**1. Toast the Rice:**

1. **Heat Oil:**
   - In a medium saucepan or deep skillet, heat the vegetable oil over medium heat.
2. **Toast Rice:**
   - Add the rice to the hot oil. Cook, stirring frequently, until the rice becomes golden brown and slightly toasted, about 5-7 minutes.

**2. Sauté Aromatics:**

1. **Add Onion and Garlic:**
   - Add the finely chopped onion to the toasted rice and cook until the onion is softened and translucent, about 3-4 minutes.
   - Stir in the minced garlic and cook for another minute, until fragrant.

**3. Add Tomatoes and Seasonings:**

1. **Stir in Tomatoes:**
   - Add the diced tomatoes (with their juices) to the saucepan. Stir well to combine with the rice.
2. **Add Spices and Liquids:**

- Stir in the ground cumin, chili powder (if using), paprika, bay leaf, salt, and black pepper.
- Pour in the chicken broth and water. Stir to combine.

### 4. Cook the Rice:

1. **Simmer:**
   - Bring the mixture to a boil, then reduce the heat to low. Cover the saucepan with a lid and simmer for about 20-25 minutes, or until the rice is tender and the liquid has been absorbed.
2. **Check and Fluff:**
   - Once the rice is cooked, remove the bay leaf. Fluff the rice with a fork.
3. **Add Peas (Optional):**
   - If using frozen peas, stir them in during the last 5 minutes of cooking. They will heat through and add a pop of color.

### 5. Garnish and Serve:

1. **Garnish:**
   - Stir in the chopped fresh cilantro if desired.
2. **Serve:**
   - Serve the Mexican rice warm as a side dish with your favorite Mexican meals, such as tacos, enchiladas, or grilled meats.

## Tips:

- **Rice Type:** Long-grain white rice is preferred for this recipe, but you can use other types of rice if necessary. Just be sure to adjust the cooking time and liquid amounts as needed.
- **Broth:** Using chicken broth adds more flavor, but vegetable broth or even water can be used for a lighter option.
- **Texture:** For a fluffier texture, avoid stirring the rice too much during cooking. Just let it sit and steam once the lid is on.

Enjoy your flavorful and colorful Mexican rice, a perfect complement to any Mexican meal!

**Refried Beans**

## Ingredients

- 2 cups dried pinto beans (or black beans, if preferred)
- 1/2 onion, chopped
- 2 cloves garlic, minced
- 2 tablespoons vegetable oil (or lard, for a more traditional flavor)
- 1 teaspoon ground cumin
- 1/2 teaspoon chili powder (optional, for extra flavor)
- Salt and black pepper to taste
- 2-3 cups water (or more as needed)
- 1/2 cup chicken or vegetable broth (optional, for extra flavor)
- 1/4 cup chopped fresh cilantro (optional, for garnish)

## Instructions

**1. Prepare the Beans:**

1. **Rinse and Soak:**
   - Rinse the dried beans under cold water to remove any dirt or debris.
   - Place the beans in a large bowl and cover with water. Soak the beans overnight, or for at least 6-8 hours. Alternatively, you can use the quick-soak method: cover the beans with water, bring to a boil, then remove from heat and let them soak for 1 hour.
2. **Drain and Rinse:**
   - After soaking, drain the beans and rinse them again under cold water.

**2. Cook the Beans:**

1. **Cook Beans:**
   - In a large pot, add the soaked and rinsed beans. Cover with fresh water (about 2-3 inches above the beans).
   - Bring to a boil over high heat. Reduce the heat to low, cover, and simmer until the beans are tender, about 1-1.5 hours. You may need to add more water during cooking to keep the beans covered.
2. **Drain Beans:**
   - Once the beans are tender, drain them, reserving some of the cooking liquid.

**3. Prepare the Refried Beans:**

1. **Sauté Aromatics:**
   - In a large skillet, heat the vegetable oil or lard over medium heat.

- Add the chopped onion and cook until softened and translucent, about 4-5 minutes.
- Add the minced garlic and cook for another minute until fragrant.

2. **Mash Beans:**
   - Add the cooked beans to the skillet with the onions and garlic. Use a potato masher to mash the beans to your desired consistency. For smoother beans, you can use an immersion blender or a regular blender.
3. **Add Spices and Liquids:**
   - Stir in the ground cumin, chili powder (if using), salt, and black pepper.
   - Gradually add some of the reserved bean cooking liquid or chicken/vegetable broth to achieve the desired consistency. Continue to cook the beans, stirring frequently, until they reach your preferred thickness. You may need to add more liquid if the beans get too thick.
4. **Adjust Seasoning:**
   - Taste the refried beans and adjust seasoning as needed.

### 4. Garnish and Serve:

1. **Garnish:**
   - If desired, stir in chopped fresh cilantro for added flavor.
2. **Serve:**
   - Serve the refried beans warm as a side dish or as part of various Mexican dishes such as tacos, burritos, or enchiladas.

## Tips:

- **Consistency:** Refried beans can be as smooth or as chunky as you like. Adjust the mashing and liquid to achieve your preferred texture.
- **Fat:** For a richer flavor, lard is traditional, but vegetable oil works well too. You can also use bacon fat for extra depth.
- **Freezing:** Refried beans freeze well. Store them in an airtight container in the freezer for up to 3 months. Reheat thoroughly before serving.

Enjoy your homemade refried beans, a versatile and tasty addition to your Mexican meals!

**Salsa Roja**

## Ingredients

- **4-5 ripe tomatoes** (about 1 lb or 450 g)
- **2-3 dried guajillo chiles** (or 1-2 tablespoons guajillo chili powder)
- **1-2 dried ancho chiles** (or 1-2 tablespoons ancho chili powder)
- **1 small onion**, chopped
- **2 cloves garlic**, minced
- **1-2 tablespoons vegetable oil**
- **1 teaspoon ground cumin**
- **1/2 teaspoon dried oregano** (Mexican oregano is ideal)
- **Salt and black pepper** to taste
- **1 tablespoon lime juice** (optional, for added brightness)
- **1/4 cup chopped fresh cilantro** (optional, for garnish)

## Instructions

**1. Prepare the Chiles:**

1. **Toast Chiles:**
    - Heat a dry skillet over medium heat. Add the dried guajillo and ancho chiles. Toast them lightly, turning occasionally, until fragrant, about 1-2 minutes. Be careful not to burn them.
2. **Soak Chiles:**
    - Place the toasted chiles in a bowl and cover with hot water. Let them soak for about 15 minutes until they become soft. Drain and remove the stems and seeds.

**2. Make the Salsa:**

1. **Cook Vegetables:**
    - In a large skillet, heat the vegetable oil over medium heat.
    - Add the chopped onion and cook until softened and translucent, about 5 minutes.
    - Add the minced garlic and cook for another minute until fragrant.
2. **Blend Ingredients:**
    - In a blender or food processor, combine the soaked chiles, tomatoes (cut into chunks), cooked onion, and garlic. Blend until smooth. If the mixture is too thick, you can add a little water to help blend it.
3. **Cook the Salsa:**
    - Return the blended salsa to the skillet. Stir in the ground cumin, dried oregano, salt, and black pepper.

- Simmer over medium heat for about 10-15 minutes, stirring occasionally, until the salsa thickens and the flavors meld together. Taste and adjust seasoning as needed.
4. **Finish and Garnish:**
   - If desired, stir in lime juice for a touch of brightness.
   - Garnish with chopped fresh cilantro if you like.

## 3. Serve:

1. **Serve Warm or Cold:**
   - The salsa can be served warm or allowed to cool to room temperature. It's great with tortilla chips, tacos, burritos, or as a condiment for many Mexican dishes.

## Tips:

- **Chili Powder:** If using chili powders instead of dried chiles, adjust the amount based on your heat preference and the strength of the chili powder.
- **Texture:** Adjust the blending time based on your preferred salsa texture. For a chunkier salsa, blend for less time or pulse lightly.
- **Storage:** Salsa Roja can be stored in an airtight container in the refrigerator for up to one week. It can also be frozen for up to 3 months.

Enjoy your homemade Salsa Roja, a versatile and flavorful addition to your meals!

**Pico de Gallo**

## Ingredients

- 4-5 ripe tomatoes, finely diced
- 1 small onion, finely chopped
- 1-2 jalapeños, seeds removed and finely diced (adjust to taste for heat level)
- 1/4 cup chopped fresh cilantro
- 1-2 tablespoons lime juice (to taste)
- Salt and black pepper to taste

## Instructions

### 1. Prepare the Ingredients:

1. **Dice Tomatoes:**
   - Wash and dice the tomatoes into small, bite-sized pieces. If you prefer a less watery salsa, you can remove some of the seeds before dicing.
2. **Chop Onion and Jalapeños:**
   - Finely chop the onion and jalapeños. Adjust the amount of jalapeños based on your desired level of spiciness.
3. **Chop Cilantro:**
   - Roughly chop the fresh cilantro leaves.

### 2. Combine Ingredients:

1. **Mix in a Bowl:**
   - In a medium bowl, combine the diced tomatoes, chopped onion, diced jalapeños, and chopped cilantro.
2. **Season:**
   - Add lime juice, salt, and black pepper. Stir well to combine all the ingredients.

### 3. Adjust Flavor:

1. **Taste and Adjust:**
   - Taste the pico de gallo and adjust the seasoning as needed. You can add more lime juice for extra tang, more salt, or more jalapeños for additional heat.

### 4. Serve:

1. **Chill (Optional):**
   - For the best flavor, let the pico de gallo sit for about 15-30 minutes to allow the flavors to meld together. However, it can be served immediately.
2. **Enjoy:**

- Serve pico de gallo as a dip with tortilla chips, or as a fresh topping for tacos, grilled meats, or any other dish where a burst of freshness is desired.

## Tips:

- **Ripeness:** Use ripe, juicy tomatoes for the best flavor and texture.
- **Heat Level:** Adjust the number of jalapeños to control the spiciness of the salsa. For a milder version, you can remove the seeds and membranes from the jalapeños or use milder chili peppers.
- **Texture:** Pico de gallo is typically chunky. If you prefer a smoother texture, you can pulse it briefly in a food processor, but be careful not to over-process.

Enjoy your homemade Pico de Gallo, a simple yet flavorful addition to your meals that brings a fresh and zesty kick!

**Albondigas (Mexican Meatballs)**

# Ingredients

**For the Meatballs:**

- 1 lb (450 g) ground beef (or a mix of beef and pork)
- 1/2 cup cooked rice (white or brown)
- 1/4 cup finely chopped onion
- 1/4 cup chopped fresh cilantro
- 1 large egg
- 2 cloves garlic, minced
- 1 teaspoon ground cumin
- 1/2 teaspoon dried oregano (Mexican oregano is ideal)
- 1/2 teaspoon chili powder (optional, for extra flavor)
- Salt and black pepper to taste

**For the Broth:**

- 1 tablespoon vegetable oil
- 1 small onion, chopped
- 2 cloves garlic, minced
- 1 can (14.5 oz) diced tomatoes (or 1 1/2 cups fresh tomatoes, finely chopped)
- 4 cups beef or chicken broth
- 1-2 carrots, peeled and sliced
- 1-2 potatoes, peeled and cubed (optional)
- 1/2 cup frozen peas (optional)
- 1 bay leaf
- 1 teaspoon ground cumin
- 1/2 teaspoon dried oregano
- Salt and black pepper to taste
- Chopped fresh cilantro (for garnish)
- Lime wedges (for serving)

# Instructions

**1. Prepare the Meatballs:**

1. **Mix Ingredients:**
   - In a large bowl, combine the ground meat, cooked rice, chopped onion, cilantro, egg, minced garlic, ground cumin, dried oregano, chili powder (if using), salt, and black pepper. Mix until well combined.
2. **Form Meatballs:**

- Shape the mixture into meatballs, about 1 to 1.5 inches in diameter. You should get about 20-24 meatballs, depending on size.

## 2. Prepare the Broth:

1. **Sauté Aromatics:**
   - In a large pot, heat the vegetable oil over medium heat.
   - Add the chopped onion and cook until softened, about 5 minutes.
   - Add the minced garlic and cook for another minute until fragrant.
2. **Add Tomatoes:**
   - Stir in the diced tomatoes and cook for about 3 minutes, allowing the flavors to meld.
3. **Add Broth and Vegetables:**
   - Pour in the beef or chicken broth. Add the sliced carrots, cubed potatoes (if using), bay leaf, ground cumin, dried oregano, salt, and black pepper.
   - Bring the mixture to a boil, then reduce the heat to a simmer.

## 3. Cook the Meatballs:

1. **Add Meatballs to Broth:**
   - Carefully add the meatballs to the simmering broth. Make sure the meatballs are not crowded; you may need to cook them in batches.
2. **Simmer:**
   - Simmer the meatballs in the broth for about 25-30 minutes, or until they are cooked through and the vegetables are tender. If using frozen peas, add them during the last 5 minutes of cooking.

## 4. Finish and Serve:

1. **Garnish:**
   - Remove the bay leaf. Stir in chopped fresh cilantro if desired.
2. **Serve:**
   - Serve the albondigas hot, with lime wedges on the side for squeezing over the meatballs. You can also serve with warm tortillas or crusty bread.

## Tips:

- **Rice:** The rice in the meatballs helps to keep them tender and adds texture. You can use leftover rice for convenience.
- **Vegetables:** Feel free to adjust the vegetables based on your preference or what you have on hand. Other vegetables like corn or green beans can also be added.
- **Broth:** For a richer broth, you can use homemade beef broth or chicken broth. Adjust the seasoning to taste.

Enjoy your homemade Albondigas, a hearty and flavorful dish that's perfect for family dinners and gatherings!

**Chimichangas**

## Ingredients

### For the Filling:

- 1 lb (450 g) ground beef (or chicken, pork, or a combination)
- 1 small onion, chopped
- 2 cloves garlic, minced
- 1 cup cooked beans (pinto, black beans, or refried beans)
- 1 cup shredded cheese (cheddar, Monterey Jack, or a Mexican blend)
- 1/2 cup salsa (store-bought or homemade)
- 1 tablespoon chili powder
- 1 teaspoon ground cumin
- 1/2 teaspoon paprika
- Salt and black pepper to taste

### For the Chimichangas:

- 4 large flour tortillas
- Vegetable oil (for frying)
- 1 cup shredded lettuce (for garnish, optional)
- 1/2 cup chopped tomatoes (for garnish, optional)
- 1/4 cup chopped fresh cilantro (for garnish, optional)
- Sour cream, salsa, and guacamole (for serving)

## Instructions

### 1. Prepare the Filling:

1. **Cook Meat:**
   - In a large skillet over medium heat, cook the ground beef (or your choice of meat) until browned. Break it up with a spoon as it cooks.
2. **Sauté Aromatics:**
   - Add the chopped onion and cook until softened, about 5 minutes. Stir in the minced garlic and cook for another minute.
3. **Add Seasonings and Beans:**
   - Stir in the chili powder, ground cumin, paprika, salt, and black pepper. Mix well.
   - Add the cooked beans and salsa to the skillet. Stir until well combined and heated through. Remove from heat and set aside.
4. **Add Cheese:**
   - Stir in the shredded cheese until it melts into the filling mixture.

**2. Assemble the Chimichangas:**

1. **Heat Tortillas:**
   - Warm the flour tortillas in a dry skillet or microwave until they are pliable. This makes them easier to fold and roll.
2. **Fill Tortillas:**
   - Place about 1/2 cup of the filling in the center of each tortilla.
3. **Roll and Fold:**
   - Fold the sides of the tortilla over the filling, then roll up the tortilla from the bottom to enclose the filling completely, making a tight cylinder.

**3. Fry the Chimichangas:**

1. **Heat Oil:**
   - In a deep skillet or frying pan, heat about 1-2 inches of vegetable oil over medium-high heat until it reaches 350°F (175°C). You can test the oil temperature by dropping a small piece of tortilla into the oil; it should bubble and float.
2. **Fry Chimichangas:**
   - Carefully add the chimichangas to the hot oil, seam side down. Fry them in batches, if necessary, to avoid overcrowding the pan. Fry until golden brown and crispy, about 3-4 minutes per side.
3. **Drain:**
   - Use a slotted spoon to remove the chimichangas from the oil and drain them on paper towels to remove excess oil.

**4. Serve:**

1. **Garnish:**
   - Serve the chimichangas hot, garnished with shredded lettuce, chopped tomatoes, and fresh cilantro if desired.
2. **Accompaniments:**
   - Serve with sour cream, salsa, and guacamole on the side.

## Tips:

- **Fillings:** You can customize the filling with other ingredients like sautéed peppers, corn, or different types of cheese. For a vegetarian version, use beans and cheese or add sautéed vegetables.
- **Oil Temperature:** Ensure the oil is hot enough before adding the chimichangas to achieve a crispy texture. If the oil is not hot enough, the chimichangas will absorb more oil and become greasy.
- **Baking Option:** For a lighter version, you can bake the chimichangas. Place them seam side down on a baking sheet, brush with oil, and bake in a preheated oven at 400°F (200°C) for 20-25 minutes, or until crispy and golden brown.

Enjoy your homemade chimichangas, a crispy and flavorful treat that's perfect for any meal or special occasion!

**Mexican Cornbread**

## Ingredients

- **1 cup cornmeal**
- **1 cup all-purpose flour**
- **1/4 cup sugar** (adjust to taste)
- **1 tablespoon baking powder**
- **1/2 teaspoon salt**
- **1 cup milk**
- **1/4 cup vegetable oil** (or melted butter)
- **2 large eggs**
- **1 cup shredded cheese** (cheddar, Monterey Jack, or a Mexican blend)
- **1-2 jalapeños**, finely chopped (seeds removed for less heat)
- **1/4 cup chopped fresh cilantro** (optional, for added flavor)
- **1/2 cup frozen or fresh corn kernels** (optional, for added texture)

## Instructions

**1. Preheat Oven and Prepare Pan:**

1. **Preheat Oven:**
   - Preheat your oven to 400°F (200°C).
2. **Prepare Pan:**
   - Grease a 9-inch square baking pan, 8-inch round cake pan, or a cast-iron skillet.

**2. Mix Dry Ingredients:**

1. **Combine Ingredients:**
   - In a large bowl, whisk together the cornmeal, flour, sugar, baking powder, and salt.

**3. Mix Wet Ingredients:**

1. **Combine Wet Ingredients:**
   - In a separate bowl, whisk together the milk, vegetable oil (or melted butter), and eggs.
2. **Combine Wet and Dry Ingredients:**
   - Pour the wet ingredients into the dry ingredients. Stir until just combined. Do not overmix.

**4. Add Mix-ins:**

1. **Fold in Cheese and Jalapeños:**

- Gently fold in the shredded cheese, chopped jalapeños, cilantro (if using), and corn kernels (if using).

## 5. Bake:

1. **Pour Batter:**
   - Pour the batter into the prepared baking pan or skillet, spreading it evenly.
2. **Bake:**
   - Bake in the preheated oven for 20-25 minutes, or until the top is golden brown and a toothpick inserted into the center comes out clean.

## 6. Cool and Serve:

1. **Cool Slightly:**
   - Allow the cornbread to cool in the pan for about 10 minutes before cutting into squares or wedges.
2. **Serve:**
   - Serve warm or at room temperature. Mexican cornbread is delicious on its own or with a variety of toppings such as honey butter, salsa, or additional cheese.

## Tips:

- **Heat Level:** Adjust the amount of jalapeños according to your taste. If you prefer a milder cornbread, you can omit the jalapeños or use less.
- **Cheese:** Experiment with different types of cheese to find your favorite combination. A mix of cheddar and Monterey Jack is a popular choice.
- **Add-ins:** Feel free to add other ingredients like cooked bacon, green onions, or diced red bell peppers for extra flavor and texture.

Enjoy your Mexican Cornbread, a tasty and versatile side dish that adds a bit of flair to any meal!

**Enchilada Sauce**

## Ingredients

- **4-6 dried chiles** (such as guajillo, ancho, or pasilla; use a combination for depth of flavor)
- **2 tablespoons vegetable oil**
- **1 small onion**, chopped
- **2 cloves garlic**, minced
- **1 cup tomato sauce** (or 1 can, about 8 oz)
- **2 cups chicken or vegetable broth**
- **1 tablespoon chili powder**
- **1 teaspoon ground cumin**
- **1/2 teaspoon dried oregano** (Mexican oregano is ideal)
- **1/2 teaspoon paprika**
- **Salt and black pepper** to taste
- **1 teaspoon sugar** (optional, to balance acidity)
- **1 tablespoon cornstarch** (optional, for thickening; mix with 2 tablespoons water)

## Instructions

**1. Prepare the Chiles:**

1. **Toast Chiles:**
   - In a dry skillet over medium heat, lightly toast the dried chiles until they become fragrant, about 1-2 minutes. Be careful not to burn them.
2. **Soak Chiles:**
   - Remove the stems and seeds from the chiles. Place them in a bowl and cover with hot water. Let them soak for about 15 minutes until they are softened.
3. **Blend Chiles:**
   - Drain the chiles and place them in a blender or food processor. Blend with a little water until smooth. You should have about 1/2 cup of chile paste.

**2. Cook the Sauce:**

1. **Sauté Aromatics:**
   - In a medium saucepan, heat the vegetable oil over medium heat.
   - Add the chopped onion and cook until softened, about 5 minutes.
   - Stir in the minced garlic and cook for another minute until fragrant.
2. **Add Chile Paste:**
   - Stir in the chile paste and cook for 2-3 minutes to blend the flavors.
3. **Add Tomato Sauce and Broth:**
   - Stir in the tomato sauce and chicken or vegetable broth. Mix well to combine.

4. **Add Spices:**
   - Stir in the chili powder, ground cumin, dried oregano, paprika, salt, and black pepper.
5. **Simmer:**
   - Bring the sauce to a simmer. Reduce the heat to low and cook for 15-20 minutes, stirring occasionally, until the sauce thickens and the flavors meld together.
6. **Thicken (Optional):**
   - If you prefer a thicker sauce, mix the cornstarch with 2 tablespoons of water to form a slurry. Stir it into the sauce and cook for an additional 2-3 minutes until thickened.

### 3. Adjust Seasoning:

1. **Taste and Adjust:**
   - Taste the enchilada sauce and adjust the seasoning as needed. You can add a teaspoon of sugar if the sauce is too acidic or adjust the salt and pepper to taste.

### 4. Serve:

1. **Use or Store:**
   - Use the sauce immediately for enchiladas, or let it cool and store it in an airtight container in the refrigerator for up to a week. It can also be frozen for up to 3 months.

## Tips:

- **Chili Variations:** Experiment with different types of dried chiles for varying levels of heat and flavor. Guajillo chiles give a mild, sweet flavor, while ancho chiles add depth.
- **Adjusting Heat:** If you prefer a spicier sauce, you can add a pinch of cayenne pepper or increase the amount of chili powder.
- **Blender:** Make sure to blend the chiles thoroughly to ensure a smooth sauce. You can add a bit of soaking water to the blender if needed.

Enjoy your homemade enchilada sauce, perfect for smothering enchiladas, tacos, or any dish that needs a flavorful kick!

**Mexican Stuffed Peppers**

## Ingredients

- 4 large bell peppers (any color)
- 1 lb (450 g) ground beef (or ground turkey, chicken, or pork)
- 1 small onion, chopped
- 2 cloves garlic, minced
- 1 cup cooked rice (white or brown)
- 1 can (15 oz) black beans, drained and rinsed
- 1 cup corn kernels (fresh, frozen, or canned)
- 1 cup shredded cheese (cheddar, Monterey Jack, or a Mexican blend)
- 1 cup salsa (store-bought or homemade)
- 1 tablespoon chili powder
- 1 teaspoon ground cumin
- 1/2 teaspoon paprika
- Salt and black pepper to taste
- 2 tablespoons vegetable oil
- Chopped fresh cilantro (optional, for garnish)
- Lime wedges (optional, for serving)

## Instructions

### 1. Prepare the Peppers:

1. **Preheat Oven:**
   - Preheat your oven to 375°F (190°C).
2. **Prepare Peppers:**
   - Wash and cut the tops off the bell peppers. Remove the seeds and membranes from the inside of the peppers. Set aside.

### 2. Cook the Filling:

1. **Sauté Meat:**
   - In a large skillet, heat the vegetable oil over medium heat.
   - Add the chopped onion and cook until softened, about 5 minutes.
   - Add the minced garlic and cook for another minute until fragrant.
   - Add the ground beef (or other ground meat) and cook until browned, breaking it up with a spoon as it cooks. Drain any excess fat.
2. **Add Seasonings:**
   - Stir in the chili powder, ground cumin, paprika, salt, and black pepper. Mix well.
3. **Combine Ingredients:**
   - Add the cooked rice, black beans, corn, and 1/2 cup of the shredded cheese to the skillet. Stir until combined and heated through. Remove from heat.

### 3. Stuff the Peppers:

1. **Fill Peppers:**
   - Spoon the filling mixture into each bell pepper, packing it down slightly. Place the stuffed peppers in a baking dish.
2. **Add Salsa:**
   - Pour the salsa over the stuffed peppers, allowing it to seep into the bottom of the baking dish.

### 4. Bake:

1. **Bake Peppers:**
   - Cover the baking dish with aluminum foil and bake in the preheated oven for 30 minutes.
2. **Add Cheese:**
   - Remove the foil and sprinkle the remaining 1/2 cup of shredded cheese over the tops of the stuffed peppers.
   - Return to the oven and bake for an additional 10-15 minutes, or until the peppers are tender and the cheese is melted and bubbly.

### 5. Serve:

1. **Garnish:**
   - Remove the peppers from the oven and let them cool slightly before serving.
   - Garnish with chopped fresh cilantro if desired.
2. **Enjoy:**
   - Serve the Mexican stuffed peppers with lime wedges on the side for added flavor. They make a great standalone meal or can be paired with a side of Mexican rice or a fresh salad.

## Tips:

- **Meat Alternatives:** You can substitute the ground beef with ground turkey, chicken, or pork, or make them vegetarian by using more beans and vegetables.
- **Cheese:** Feel free to use your favorite cheese or a mix of cheeses for extra flavor.
- **Spice Level:** Adjust the amount of chili powder and other spices to match your heat preference. If you like it spicier, you can also add some chopped jalapeños to the filling.

Enjoy your Mexican Stuffed Peppers, a tasty and hearty dish that brings vibrant Mexican flavors to your table!

**Baked Mexican Chicken**

## Ingredients

- 4 boneless, skinless chicken breasts (or thighs, if preferred)
- 1 tablespoon vegetable oil
- 1 tablespoon chili powder
- 1 teaspoon ground cumin
- 1 teaspoon smoked paprika (or regular paprika)
- 1/2 teaspoon garlic powder
- 1/2 teaspoon onion powder
- 1/2 teaspoon dried oregano (Mexican oregano is ideal)
- 1/2 teaspoon salt
- 1/4 teaspoon black pepper
- 1/2 cup salsa (store-bought or homemade)
- 1/2 cup shredded cheese (cheddar, Monterey Jack, or a Mexican blend)
- 1 lime, cut into wedges (for serving)
- Chopped fresh cilantro (optional, for garnish)

## Instructions

**1. Preheat Oven:**

1. **Preheat Oven:**
    - Preheat your oven to 375°F (190°C).

**2. Prepare the Chicken:**

1. **Season Chicken:**
    - In a small bowl, mix together the chili powder, ground cumin, smoked paprika, garlic powder, onion powder, dried oregano, salt, and black pepper.
    - Rub the spice mixture evenly over the chicken breasts.
2. **Sear Chicken (Optional):**
    - For added flavor, heat the vegetable oil in a skillet over medium-high heat. Sear the chicken breasts for about 2-3 minutes per side, until golden brown. This step is optional but helps to lock in flavor and juiciness.

**3. Bake the Chicken:**

1. **Place Chicken in Baking Dish:**
    - Arrange the seasoned chicken breasts in a baking dish.
2. **Add Salsa:**
    - Spoon the salsa evenly over the chicken breasts.

3. **Bake:**
   - Bake in the preheated oven for 25-30 minutes, or until the chicken reaches an internal temperature of 165°F (74°C) and is cooked through.
4. **Add Cheese:**
   - During the last 5 minutes of baking, sprinkle the shredded cheese over the chicken and return to the oven until the cheese is melted and bubbly.

## 4. Serve:

1. **Garnish:**
   - Remove the chicken from the oven and let it rest for a few minutes before serving.
   - Garnish with chopped fresh cilantro, if desired.
2. **Enjoy:**
   - Serve the Baked Mexican Chicken with lime wedges on the side. It pairs well with rice, beans, or a fresh salad.

## Tips:

- **Marinate:** For even more flavor, you can marinate the chicken in the spice mixture and salsa for at least 30 minutes or overnight in the refrigerator.
- **Veggies:** You can add vegetables like sliced bell peppers or onions to the baking dish for a complete meal.
- **Cheese:** Feel free to use your favorite type of cheese or a combination of cheeses.

This Baked Mexican Chicken is a simple yet delicious way to enjoy Mexican flavors with minimal effort. Enjoy!

**Mexican Shrimp Cocktail**

## Ingredients

- 1 lb (450 g) large shrimp, peeled and deveined
- 1/2 cup ketchup
- 1/2 cup tomato sauce
- 1/4 cup freshly squeezed lime juice (about 2 limes)
- 1/4 cup chopped fresh cilantro
- 1 small red onion, finely chopped
- 1-2 jalapeños, finely chopped (adjust to taste for heat)
- 1 cup diced cucumber (optional, for extra crunch)
- 1 avocado, diced (for garnish)
- Salt and black pepper to taste
- Tortilla chips or tostadas (for serving)

## Instructions

### 1. Cook the Shrimp:

1. **Boil Shrimp:**
   - In a large pot of salted water, bring to a boil. Add the shrimp and cook for 2-3 minutes until they turn pink and opaque.
   - Immediately transfer the shrimp to a bowl of ice water to stop cooking. Drain and pat dry.

### 2. Prepare the Cocktail Sauce:

1. **Mix Ingredients:**
   - In a large bowl, combine the ketchup, tomato sauce, lime juice, chopped cilantro, finely chopped red onion, and jalapeños. Stir well to mix.
2. **Season:**
   - Season the sauce with salt and black pepper to taste.

### 3. Combine Shrimp and Sauce:

1. **Add Shrimp:**
   - Add the cooked shrimp to the cocktail sauce and mix until the shrimp are well coated.
2. **Add Cucumber (Optional):**
   - If using, fold in the diced cucumber for added crunch.

### 4. Chill:

1. **Refrigerate:**
   - Cover the bowl and refrigerate for at least 30 minutes to allow the flavors to meld together.

**5. Serve:**

1. **Garnish:**
   - Just before serving, gently fold in the diced avocado.
2. **Serve:**
   - Serve the Mexican Shrimp Cocktail in individual bowls or glasses with tortilla chips or tostadas on the side.

## Tips:

- **Heat Level:** Adjust the amount of jalapeños to control the spiciness. You can also remove the seeds and membranes for a milder heat.
- **Freshness:** For the best flavor, use fresh lime juice and adjust the seasoning as needed.
- **Garnishes:** Feel free to add extra garnishes like chopped cilantro or lime wedges for additional flavor.

Enjoy your refreshing and flavorful Mexican Shrimp Cocktail!

www.ingramcontent.com/pod-product-compliance
Lightning Source LLC
LaVergne TN
LVHW081556060526
838201LV00054B/1915